100 MORE SWIMMING DRILLS

# 100 MORE SWIMMING DRILLS

*by Blythe Lucero*

*Dedicated to PB*
*Special spirit, special soul*

Meyer & Meyer Sport

British Library Cataloguing in Publication Data
A catalogue record for this book is available from the British Library

**100 More Swimming Drills**
Maidenhead: Meyer & Meyer Sport (UK) Ltd., 2013
ISBN: 978-1-78255-001-3

© 2013 by Meyer & Meyer Sport (UK) Ltd.
Aachen, Auckland, Beirut, Budapest, Cairo, Cape Town, Dubai, Hägendorf,
Indianapolis, Maidenhead, Singapore, Sydney, Tehran, Wien

 Member of the World Sport Publishers' Association (WSPA)
www.w-s-p-a.org

Printed by: B.O.S.S Druck und Medien GmbH, Germany
ISBN: 978-1-78255-001-3
E-Mail: info@m-m-sports.com
www.m-m-sports.com

Thinkstock/iStockphoto

# TABLE OF CONTENTS

# INTRODUCTION

It was when I was about twelve, that I figured out swimming really agreed with me, and for the next twelve years competitive swimming was a central part of my life. My identity was to a large extent defined by swimming. My schedule revolved around training and swim meets. My daily routine was to rise before dawn and ride my bike, along with my sisters single file through the streets of Berkeley, California, pedaling the slight but steady uphill grade to swim practice at the YMCA where in that 20-yard basement pool we swam a two-hour workout before school, and another one after school.

I worked hard at those practices, accomplishing lots of swimming and thereby achieving a superior level of conditioning. I also developed very efficient strokes, partially by necessity–to make it through those tough practices–but also because of my coaches' focus on honing of the mechanics of swimming. In addition to the countless 200s I would do on a daily basis, there were a variety of technique drills that used to annoy me to no end. Thinking back, I can remember drills that applied to body position, kick, arm stroke and recovery, breathing, leverage and coordination. But at the time, I had no patience for drills... probably because I didn't understand them.

I was one of those "thinking swimmers" with the distinct need to understand the purpose of each set we were assigned, as opposed to the kind of swimmer who simply trusts that the coach knows best. "How exactly is this exercise going to make me a better swimmer?" I recall asking my coach, to which he would simply reply, "Ready, go!"

So I would push off and do the drill of the day, lap after lap, convinced I was wasting precious practice time, but eventually realizing improvements to my stroke

*Author Blythe Lucero as a young swimmer focuses on her race to come.*

efficiency through all that repetition. I often wonder what would have become of my swimming if I had understood the purpose of each drill before pushing off.

Now that I am coaching swimming, I make a big deal of the mind/body connection. I want each swimmer to understand the goal of every drill before doing it. I spend a lot of time defining the purpose of each exercise, describing the desired outcome so the athlete has a clear mental picture before pushing off the wall. I feel strongly that an athlete whose mind is as involved in the act of swimming as his or her body is, will improve more steadily because he or she is prepared to absorb the full benefit of the drill, and is further prepared to put into use the technique the drill brings forward.

The goal of a drill is not to do it then leave it behind, but to do it and then incorporate it into one's swimming. To best accomplish this, the swimmer has to understand what he or she is trying to achieve in the first place.

In this book the reader will find 100 swimming drills to understand and practice.

This book is a sequel to "The 100 Best Swimming Drills," (Meyer & Meyer Sport, 2006), which has been used by swimmers around the world. This second drill book follows the same format as the first and gives swimmers and coaches even more variety of drills with which to use to improve swimming technique.

This volume contains drills for each of the competitive strokes, and for specific aspects of each of these strokes. Accompanying each drill are diagrams and photos to help the swimmer visualize what the goal of the particular drill is while doing it. Drill feedback charts follow each drill to help work through rough spots.

As you work your way through the drills in this book, the key word is focus. It's all about thinking and swimming. If you find yourself losing focus, take a break. Start again later. If one drill doesn't seem to work for you, try it a few more times, but don't get frustrated and stop completely, just move on to another drill. Maybe go back to that one that you just can't get after you finish all the other drills. Every drill does not make sense to every swimmer. That is why there are a hundred drills!

*Above all, have fun becoming a better swimmer.*

# CHAPTER ONE

CHAPTER 1                                    CHAPTER 2

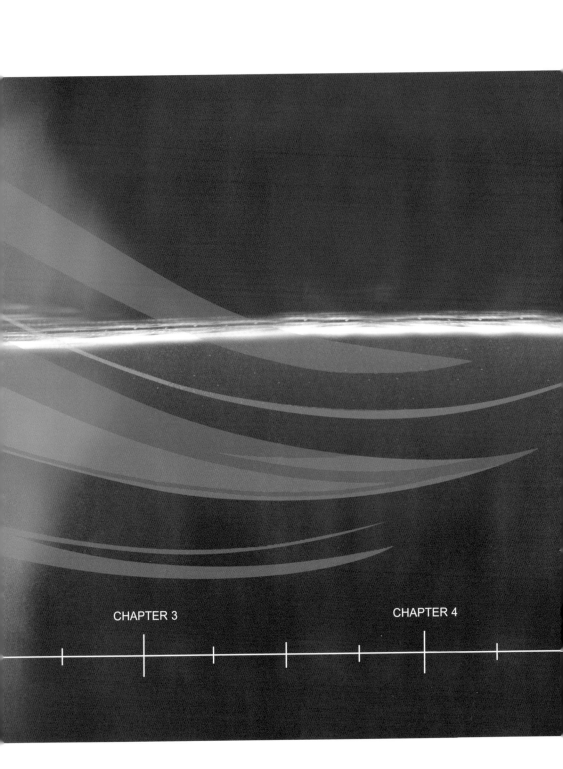

CHAPTER 3

CHAPTER 4

# HOW TO USE THIS BOOK

## START TO FINISH

This book is designed for a swimmer interested in improving his or her swimming skills all around to start at the beginning and build the various elements of one stroke, from float through coordinated action, and then move on to the next stroke, again practicing and building each element one upon another. The reader can work through the four competitive strokes, starting with freestyle, then proceed to back-stroke, breaststroke, and finally the elusive butterfly!

The strokes are presented in this order because many concepts central to the drills in the Freestyle section, including correct floatation, productive kicking and arm stroke acceleration will be helpful in achieving skills in the other strokes. In addition, although the muscle development that occurs through practicing each particular is slightly unique, practicing all the strokes gives the swimmer the most well rounded strength development that will be beneficial to swimming in general. Lastly, many swimmers will discover that a stroke they have previously avoided because it felt slow or awkward will become their new favorite stroke as they learn to perform it with the correct technique and coordination.

## FOCUS ON A SINGLE STROKE

Swimmers interested in only a particular stroke can start at that stroke section and work their way through the drills pertaining to that stroke, from float to coordina-tion, simple to complex. Swimmers who want to focus on improving one certain aspect of a particular stroke, will be able to flip to that particular section and find a variety of drills to work on a certain troublesome stroke element.

Swimmers using this book in this last way will find it helpful to follow up drill practice for a particular element, such as arm stroke or kick, with the drills presented in that stroke section for leverage and coordination. The reasoning behind this is that once a swimmer improves one element of their stroke, the stroke fits together a bit differently, either because of changes in the timing or momentum. Therefore it is to the swimmer's advantage to practice putting all the stroke elements together again to get the most out of their improved skill in the area of emphasis.

## BRING THIS BOOK TO THE POOL

Whichever way you want to use this book, start by reading the drill(s) you are focusing on thoroughly. Read them more than once. Look at the diagrams and photos so you have a picture in your mind of what you are trying to do before you do it. Then take the book with you to practice. Refer to it. Get it wet!

Practice a lot. Practice over several days and weeks. Most drills are awkward, even uncomfortable at first. It is only through practice that they start to feel more natural. It is only when a drill starts feeling natural that it can start making sense and help you make improvements to your swimming.

Between practice sessions, use the Drill Feedback Charts that follow each drill, diagram and photo to work through stumbling blocks. The problems included in these charts represent the most common trouble spots that can frustrate a swimmer's progress in achieving the full benefit of a particular drill. Accompanying each common problem are modifications to help the swimmer stay on track. Remember that making modifications is part of the learning process. Quality practice is key to improving stroke technique. Strive to learn and practice each drill correctly for it to have a positive impact on your stroke. Finally, the observations and feedback of a trusted coach can be valuable in making the most out of every drill.

# CHAPTER TWO

CHAPTER 1                                    CHAPTER 2

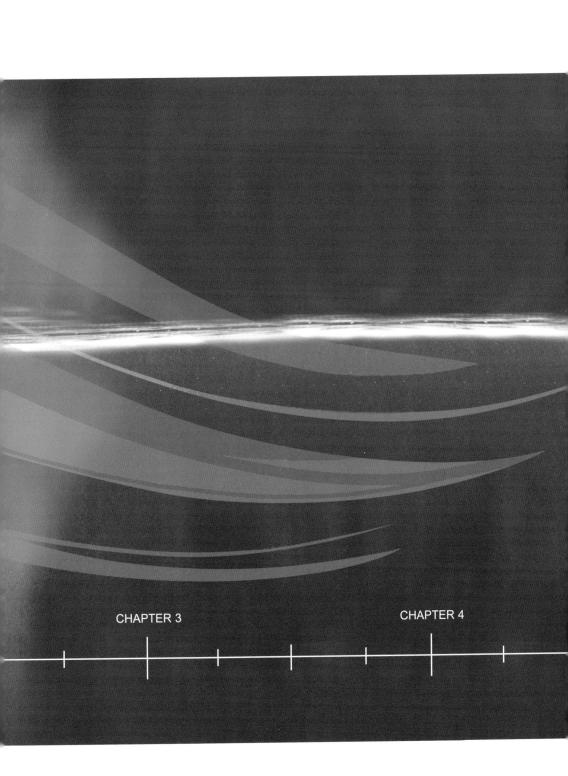

CHAPTER 3

CHAPTER 4

# THE QUEST
# FOR BETTER SWIMMING

Swimming is a sport for patient athletes. It takes time and focus to learn good technique, and time and dedication to get strong enough to maintain good technique for any distance. Instant gratification is not often experienced in competitive swimming. But, with patience, focus and dedication the rewards of better swimming will come.

## PRACTICE MAKES PERFECT?

Practice is a key element in improving swimming technique. And frequent practice has been shown to increase the rate of improvement. Further, in swimming, where forward motion is achieved through repetitive stroke actions, it is essential to use correct technique while practicing the series of actions that make up the stroke. If you practice poor stroke mechanics, you learn poor stroke mechanics. In swimming like most things, it is quite difficult to un-learn bad habits. So, the saying "practice makes perfect" is not exactly correct. What is more accurate is to say, "perfect practice makes perfect".

## WHAT'S THE POINT?

When doing drill work to improve swimming, it is very important to understand the point of each drill you are doing. Know what you are trying to achieve. Know what the drill is supposed to emphasize. Know what improvements you are supposed to feel through the drill. Focus on these things the entire time you are practicing.

Doing drill work without this focus will not help you improve effectively because you do not have a clear goal in mind. It is mindless swimming, and although sometimes it's relaxing to be on auto-pilot when you swim, you must be alert and focused to get good results from drill work.

## WHAT TO FOCUS ON

### Body Position

Body position is the foundation of good swimming. Time and effort devoted to developing the best body position possible is well spent. An ideal float eliminates a great deal of drag and positions the swimmer to get the most out of arm stroke and kick, and to produce more leverage. Without a good float position a swimmer will work harder for less return.

### Kick

Being a strong kicker makes you a stronger swimmer. Good kickers depend on flexibility and foot speed. Good kickers tend to have well developed endurance that can give them an edge. The power added to the stroke by the lower limbs can make the difference between winning a race or not. In addition the kick also adds balance to the rest of the stroke, and provides an important rhythmic element.

## Arm Stroke

In every stroke except for breaststroke, the arm stroke provides most of the potential power in swimming, making it a priority among all stroke elements to develop, refine and perfect. For the purposes of this book, when the term arm stroke is used, it refers to the propulsive part of the arm cycle, that is, the part where the arm is in the water. Key points of the arm stroke include the catch, the path of the hand, elbow position and acceleration from front to back. These are some of the primary elements of the arm stroke that affect swimming efficiency and speed. As well as forward motion, the arm stroke contributes to stroke alignment and balance to the rest of the swimming effort.

## Recovery

The arm stroke recovery is an often-misunderstood element of the swimming stroke. While the recovery is the most visible part of the arm stroke, as it happens out of the water (except for breaststroke), its contribution to forward motion is minor. Therefore spending a great deal of time and attention fashioning the look of this part of the stroke is not a high priority. Instead, attention should be paid to the balancing effect that the recovery has on the rest of the stroke. In addition, as the name "recovery" implies, this is the time that the arms can rest, so developing a relaxed recovery where rest can truly be achieved should be a main focus.

## Breathing

Breathing in swimming, like any athletic effort is essential to keep the muscles fueled. But more so than any other sport, breathing while swimming is limited by the fact that the face is mostly in the water. Therefore breathing in swimming must become an integral part of the stroke action, incorporated seamlessly into the line of the stroke. Because poor breathing technique can halt forward motion by inter-rupting the flow of the stroke, it should be a priority to develop good breathing technique that works within the silhouette and rhythm of the stroke.

## Leverage

Unique to our sport is the way swimmers create forward motion from a floating position, without the benefit of the ground used by land athletes to provide stability and to create traction. Swimmers must create the leverage effect within their bodies and learn to produce effective and ongoing leverage to realize the most efficient forward motion while floating.

## Coordination

The effectiveness of the many actions of swimming can either enhance each other or fight each other. The best swimmers have discovered how to sequence and combine these various actions so that each individual action works in a chain reaction to enhance the way the body moves forward in the water.

## IS YOUR TECHNIQUE "GOOD ENOUGH?"

I have frequently heard, "I just wanna swim!" as a coach. Some swimmers choose to skip over drill work either due to time constraints, or because they think that conditioning is a more important use of their time. Others view their swimming time as a chance to relax. The problem is that due to the repetitive nature of swimming, imperfect technique practiced again and again becomes habit, and can slow a swimmer's progress, and even keep the swimmer from reaching his or her potential.

In addition, stroke problems are a main cause of injury in swimmers. Even the most developed swimmer has stroke flaws that, if repeated over and over, can cause injury. For the same reason, it is very important that less experienced swimmers learn correct technique and practice swimming correctly before they try to tackle big workouts. Everyone can improve their swimming technique... and everyone should, both to see their full potential, and, to avoid developing a technique-based injury that can keep a swimmer out of the pool for months.

## EXPERIENCE THE PROCESS

The process of improving your swimming requires patience. Improvements rarely happen instantaneously. For those of us who are looking for instant gratification, this may be a challenge. Often it takes several days or even weeks of repeating a drill, or series of drills before you see and feel results. During those days or weeks frequent practice is an important part of the learning process. Keep a clear picture in your mind of what you are trying to achieve. Think about it while you are performing the drills, and again afterwards.

All the time you devote to technique drills is cumulative. One day's work will build a foundation for the next day's work. Be determined in your quest, and be sure to celebrate every breakthrough!

# CHAPTER THREE

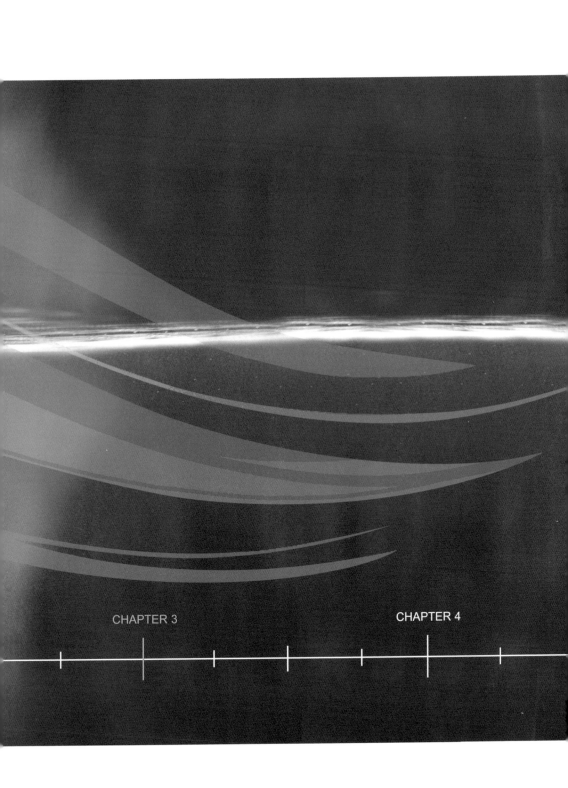

CHAPTER 3

CHAPTER 4

# WHAT'S IN A DRILL?

Drill work involves performing a routine or exercise that emphasizes correct technique through repetition, exaggeration, contrast and/or example. Drills often require the swimmer to perform only a part of a swimming stroke in order to focus on a specific skill or movement.

Through practice, the drill becomes more natural for the swimmer to perform. Only at that point, can the swimmer expect it to "rub off" on their regular swimming stroke.

## WORKING WITH DRILLS

You will see quantitative change and qualitative change when working with drills. At first you may only be able to perform the drill for a few seconds.

Gradually, through practice you will find it possible to perform the same drill for several minutes at a time. Or, at first you may not even get to the end of the pool doing a drill for the first time, but over time you will be able to accomplish multiple laps. Likewise, at first a drill will be so awkward that you just don't go anywhere. Yet with patience and practice soon you will be performing the drill with ease.

Drills work over time through multiple stages of psychomotor learning. There is no set time each stage will take. Every one is different. In order, the stages are:

**Mechanics:** The step-by-step movements which, like a new dance routine, are awkward and slow at first, but through practice become more comfortable and fluid to perform

**Discovery:** The instance when you actively begin to feel the point of the drill while you are doing it

**Understanding:** The stage when you can perform the drill seamlessly with the goal clearly in mind

**Feel:** The ability to change from drill to the regular swimming stroke and hold on to the point of the drill.

**Mastery:** Swimming with improved understanding and feel, and more efficiency as a result of drill practice

## USING SWIMMING DRILLS

### In Warm Up

After loosening up the muscles with a few laps of relaxed, progressive swimming, drills can be successfully merged into the warm up. Alternating 50s of drill and swim works well. Using a series of related drills is also very beneficial to build towards an efficient stroke. Using drills within a warm up sets the tone for a quality practice session.

### As a Recovery Set

After an intense set at practice, a few easy laps are in order. At that point, a less intense recovery set should be done. This is the perfect time to fit drill work into the

workout. Not only will a drill set provide a needed break from swimming hard without wasting precious time in the water, it will also give the swimmer the opportunity to recapture his or her technique after the previous speed-centered set. Sometimes technique can be sacrificed for speed, especially at the end of a set when the swimmer is getting tired. So, using a drill set after one of these hard sets is very beneficial.

## Within Sets

Sometimes it works to incorporate drills into a regular swim set. For instance, instead of simply doing 5 x 100 freestyle, make the first lap a drill lap, but keep the same interval as you would for all regular swim. Of course only certain drills would be appropriate in this case. Some would just not work. Choose a drill that is designed to do at near swim speed, so the set will be challenging, but doable. This can be a fun and interesting way for swimmers to accomplish both conditioning work and technique work at the same time.

## Pre-Meet

Pre-meet swimming is an excellent time to bring in drills, both during taper, and within the meet day warm up. Drills bring the mind into one's swimming, and focus it on swimming right. Drills can be grounding if a swimmer gets nervous. Using a long set of drill/swim laps that include many of the drills that have been especially meaningful to swimmer is a good way to set a positive tone for the big swim.

## Off Season

Off season swimming offers a low pressure atmosphere when many swimmers are able to focus better on the technique of swimming, than during meet season. Off season is when many swimmers and coaches choose to use drill work as a primary element of their workouts.

# CHAPTER FOUR

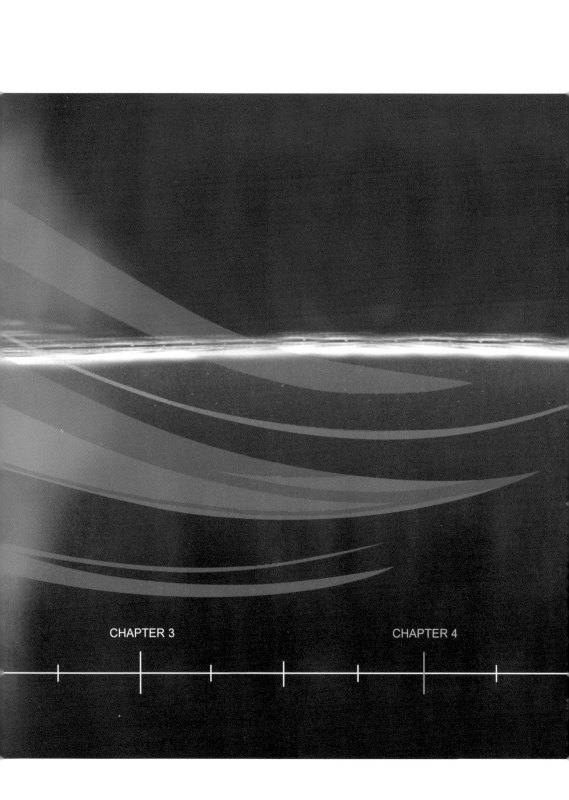

CHAPTER 3

CHAPTER 4

# 100 DRILLS

## DRILLS FOR FREESTYLE

### BODY POSITION DRILLS

Good body position in freestyle makes everything else easier. Working on how to float better in the water is not a waste of time at any level of the sport. A positive body position decreases the amount of drag a swimmer produces, improves the catch, and sets the swimmer up to get the most out of their stroke. Use the following drills to improve your body position in freestyle.

# 1. TIP FORWARD

## The purpose of this drill

- Achieving a downhill floating position
- Understanding how to change your floating position
- Avoiding drag

## How to do this drill

Step 1: Take a big breath and float face down in the water, arms at your sides.

Step 2: Notice that your chest and upper body float higher, while your legs and the lower body float lower. While this is the natural floating position for most people, it is not advantageous for swimming. It is like swimming "uphill." From this uphill position, your body bumps into a lot of water, creating drag.

*Figure 1A: The natural floating position for most people*

*Figure 1B: Tip forward by pressing down with your chest for a more advantageous floating position*

Step 3: To change this position into a more advantageous floating position, press down with your chest and feel your hips and legs rise. Practice tipping forward until you are able to achieve and maintain a downhill float, the positive body position for freestyle.

## Drill feedback chart

| PROBLEM | MODIFICATION |
| --- | --- |
| When I press down with my chest, my body bends in the middle. | Hold your core firm while you press your ribs down about two inches. Relax. |
| I run out of breath. | Simply stand up and start again. Do it as many times as you need to until you are able to achieve a positive floating position by tipping your body forward. |
| My legs still sink! | Some people with low body fat or high muscle content will find it harder to float downhill. If you are one of those people it is even more important for you to learn to positively affect your floating position. Practice more. You might also need to add a gentle kick, but remember that the purpose of the kick should not me to hold you up, but to move you forward, so work hard to perfect a positive float by pressing your chest downward. |

## 2. LATERAL BALANCE

### The purpose of this drill

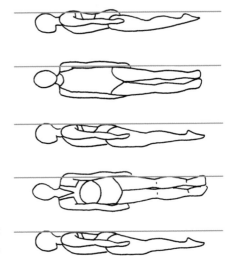

- Getting away from flat swimming
- Learning to float well while rolling
- Feeling unified power from the hips and shoulders

### How to do this drill

**Step 1:** Take a big breath and float face down in the water, arms at your sides. Achieve a downhill floating position.

*Figure 2: Achieve lateral balance*

**Step 2:** Holding your positive floating position, roll your body, but not your head to your right about 45 degrees. Your left shoulder and hip should be out of the water. Hold for the count of three.

**Step 3:** Roll your body back to your starting position, maintaining your effective, downhill position. Hold for the count of three, then roll your body, but not your head to your left about 45 degrees. Your right shoulder and hip should be out of the water. Hold for the count of three.

**Step 4:** Roll back to your starting position. Stand and get another big breath then repeat.

**Step 5:** Repeat Steps 1 - 4, adding a gentle flutter kick.

## Drill feedback chart

| PROBLEM | MODIFICATION |
| --- | --- |
| I can't seem to control my roll to 45 degrees... I just keep going. | Use your hips and shoulders to start and stop your roll. |
| I loose my downhill float very quickly when I roll. | Make sure you are looking down towards the bottom of the pool and not forward. |
| When I add the kick, I can't roll as well. | The kick should be a very gentle, quiet kick and very narrow. Make sure your hip action is connected to your roll primarily rather than to your kick. |

## **3.** STREAMLINE

### The purpose of this drill

- Learning to float tall
- Eliminating drag
- Creating a narrow silhouette

### How to do this drill

Step 1: Standing with your back against a wall, extend your arms above your head. Clasp one hand over the other, so they make a point.

Step 2: Squeezing your ears with your arms, reach higher with your hands. Press your hands, head, neck, shoulders, spine and legs into the wall.

Step 3: Holding your position against the wall, stretch your whole body upwards. Lift your ribs. Stand on your tiptoes.

*Figure 3: Streamline position*

Step 4: Get in the water and push off the wall completely underwater, immediately assuming the same position as you practiced against the wall. Be tall. Be narrow. Feel yourself cut through the water without resistance.

## Drill feedback chart

| PROBLEM | MODIFICATION |
| --- | --- |
| I can't see where I am going! | This actually means your head is positioned correctly. You should be facing the bottom of the pool, not looking forward. Yes, this makes it difficult to see where you are going. You can look forward with your eyes, put do not lift your chin. But it is best to practice this drill in un-crowded pool conditions. Also use the line on the bottom of the pool to avoid going off course. |
| I am not staying underwater well. I float to the surface quickly. | Push off a bit deeper and with much more force. The more forward motion you create, the better you will stay submerged. Also, be sure you are looking down at the bottom of the pool and not forward. |
| When I push off the wall, I end up very deep. | **Modification:** It takes practice to know your depth. Make sure your arms are correctly aligned with the rest of your body, aiming straight ahead and not downward. Your body will follow your arms, so they need to be positioned correctly as they were on the wall. |

## 4. POWER ZONE

### The purpose of this drill

- Feeling core stabilization
- Unifying the movement of the hips and shoulders
- Swimming from the core

### How to do this drill

Step 1: Stand in front of a full-length mirror. Allow your arms to hang relaxed at your sides. Draw an imaginary line connecting your left and right shoulders to your left and right hips. Within this line is your Power Zone.

Step 2: Without moving your head or feet, snap your left shoulder and hip forward about 45 degrees. Feel your right shoulder and hip snap back and equal amount as a consequence. Snap your right shoulder and hip forward and feel your left shoulder and hip snap the opposite way. Practice controlling the movement from your Power Zone.

Step 3: Begin to snap your same side shoulder and hip forward in an alternating fashion, about once per second rhythmically. Still keeping your head and feet still, feel your arms start to swing as a result of the movements of your Power Zone.

*Figure 4: The Power Zone*

Step 4: In the pool, try swimming freestyle using your Power Zone to initiate the arm stroke. Snap your right shoulder and hip forward as your right arm enters the water, and your left shoulder and hip as you left arm enters the water. Establish a rhythm and try to feel that your arm stroke initiates from the movement of your Power Zone.

## Drill feedback chart

| PROBLEM | MODIFICATION |
| --- | --- |
| I feel my shoulders doing the snap, but not my hips. | By incorporating the hips into the snap too you will be using your whole Power Zone and it will be an even stronger and more stable action. Initiate the snap from your hips, and let your shoulders follow, then your arms. Practice this in front of the mirror first, so you can get immediate feedback, then go back to the water. |
| I feel my arm stroke makes my hips and shoulders roll, not visa versa. | Because your core (Power Zone) is stronger than your arms, it is important to learn to initiate your arm stroke from the middle of your body, where you are the strongest. |
| I find myself twisting as I try to swim. | Imagine your Power Zone is made of wood. It is rigid and cannot twist or bend. Snap to the left then to the right in a unified action. Control each movement. Practice more. |

## KICK DRILLS

The flutter kick has the potential of adding significant power to the freestyle stroke. It also can use up a great deal of energy due to the amount of oxygen consumption required by the large muscles of the legs. Therefore developing an efficient flutter kick is essential in order to use your energy resources effectively. Learning to kick well should be a main priority for a better freestyle stroke. Use the following drills to improve your kicking technique for freestyle.

## 5. FISH DON'T HAVE KNEES

### The purpose of this drill

- Developing a fluid kick
- Learning to use the largest available muscles to kick
- Kicking with your whole leg

### How to do this drill

Step 1: Observe a fish moving through the water. Its movement is fluid. It uses very little energy to produce a lot of forward motion. While human swimmers are not equipped with a tail as fish are, learning to use our lower limbs like the fish uses its tail will improve our kicking. One major difference between humans and fish is that fish do not have knees, allowing them to swim without angles or loss of length as they sweep the water back and forth.

Step 2: In the water, float face down, arms at your sides and do the flutter kick. Make your kick about 12 - 15 inches wide, and mostly underwater. Produce a fluid motion that uses the entire length of the leg. Kick without creating any angles at your knees, ankles or hips. It should feel and appear as if your legs have no bones.

Step 3: Try it again. Use the large muscles your upper legs to initiate the movement of the kick, and let it flow down to your feet. Feel a fluid, wave-like kick.

*Figure 5: Kick without producing any angles at your knees, ankles and hips*

## Drill feedback chart

| PROBLEM | MODIFICATION |
|---------|--------------|
| If I don't bend my knees, my kick feels stiff. | Try using a narrower, quicker kick. Keep your legs relaxed and as long as possible. |
| I feel the kick in my calf muscles, not my upper legs. | When you point your toes, your calf muscles are engaged. Try relaxing your ankles so that the water can push your feet gently back and forth as if you are wearing long flippers. |
| My feet come completely out of the water. | This means you are raising your heels too much. This happens when your knees bend enough to make one of those angles we want to avoid. Work hard to keep your feet to connected to the water at all times. |

## 6. KICK THE BALL

### The purpose of this drill

- Knowing the range of the kick
- Understanding the kick's power phase and recovery
- Feeling the water with your feet

### How to do this drill

Step 1: Stand on the pool deck and place a ball in front of your feet. Prepare to kick the ball so it would travel about ten feet. Notice that you draw your leg back behind you as you prepare to kick the ball. Freeze at the point when your leg is drawn back to its farthest point behind you, just before you would swing it forward to kick the ball.

Step 2: Kick the ball. Freeze at the point when your leg is at its farthest point in front of you in the kick motion. Notice that it is about the same distance in front of you as it was behind you. Now, place the ball directly behind your feet. Prepare to kick the ball behind you so it travels about ten feet. Notice that it is much more difficult to accomplish than when you kicked the ball forward.

Step 3: Get in the water at a point where it is deeper than you are tall. Begin to kick flutter kick in a vertical position. Use a quick enough kicking motion to keep your face out of the water. Imagine that there is a ball in front of your foot and you are kicking it with each leg motion. Now imagine that the ball is behind you. Try kicking the ball back. Notice that it is much harder to keep your face out of the water when you are pretending to kick the ball back.

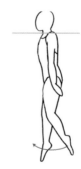

Figure 6: Kick like you are kicking a ball

47

Step 4: From your vertical position, kick flutter kick again. Experiment with a wider and narrower kick. Notice the range of motion that works best spans about 15 inches. Notice that half of that distance is behind you and half of it is in front of you.

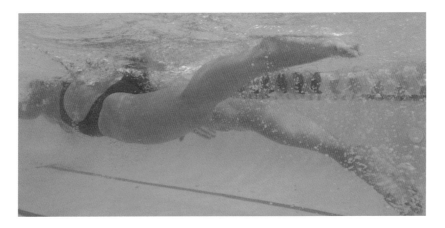

**Drill feedback chart**

| PROBLEM | MODIFICATION |
| --- | --- |
| I feel the kick in the back of my upper legs, but not the front. | You might be raising your knees when you swing your legs forward. Focus on the motion of kicking the ball forward. The power comes from the front of your upper legs, but main motion is visible in the path that your foot travels. |
| When I kick vertically, I seem to bob up and down. | Use a narrower, quicker kick. Avoid using a scissor-type kick that squeezes the legs together for power. The power of the flutter kick is in the forward motion of the kick. |
| It seems that my forward kick is quicker than my backward kick in the water. | This is exactly right! Your forward kick is the power phase and should be quick and sharp. The backward kick is the recovery, a gentler, slower motion. |

## 7. INVISIBLE KICKBOARD

### The purpose of this drill

- Developing an effective kick
- Using foot speed
- Feeling the water with the feet

### How to do this drill

Step 1: Standing in the water, stretch your arms out in front of your shoulders, and clasp your hands one over the other so they make a point in front of you. Keeping your arms in this position, lower your shoulders into the water so that your hands are at extended in front of you at the surface of the water.

Step 2: Keeping your arms in this position, lower your shoulders into the water so that your hands are at extended in front of you at the surface of the water, as if you are holding an invisible kickboard.

Step 3: Push off the wall and immediately begin kicking a quick flutter kick. Kick fast enough so that you chin remains on the surface of the water. Feel the water pushing against your feet.

Step 4: Keep kicking! Don't let your face sink. Maintain a good body position using your core to stabilize you.

*Figure 7: Invisible kickboard*

## Drill feedback chart

| PROBLEM | MODIFICATION |
|---|---|
| I sink almost as soon as I push off. | Kick faster, creating a motor effect with your feet. Press down with your chest so you are not positioned uphill. Practice more. |
| This makes my neck hurt. | It is supposed to be a challenge, but it is not supposed to hurt. Try correcting your body position so you are floating higher in the water, and try to relax your neck. If it still hurts, move on to the next drill. |
| I get tired quickly. | This drill is very difficult! The point, however is not to be able to continue it for a long time, but to feel a quick, fluid kicking while you are doing it. When you get tired, stop, rest, then start again. |

## ARM STROKE DRILLS

The freestyle arm stroke uses the entire range of the swimmer's reach from front to back, and a three-dimensional path under the water between the extremes of the reach.

The underwater phase of the arm stroke includes the entry, extension and catch, upsweep and finish, which happen in succession and with accelerating speed.

It is important to develop all of these parts to make the most effective arm stroke. Besides moving the body forward, the arm stroke also provides alignment and balance to the rest of the stroke. Use the following drills to improve your arm stroke technique for freestyle.

## **8.** OVER THE BARREL

### The purpose of this drill

- Practicing a high elbow position
- Developing a good hand entry
- Achieving a solid catch

### How to do this drill

Step 1: Stand in the water facing a lane rope. Place your right arm over the lane rope above the elbow. Extend your arm forward so it is aligned with your shoulder straight in front of you.

Step 2: From this position, start to trace the path of a freestyle stroke. With the lane line supporting your arm at the elbow, initiate the arm stroke with your hand and forearm. Notice that your elbow remains in a stable, high position through these initial stages of the underwater arm stroke.

Step 3: Try it again without the lane rope. Start your stroke with your fingertips, hand, wrist and forearm, leaving your elbow as still as possible, and higher in the water than your hand. It should feel as if your arm is going over a barrel.

Step 4: Try it again. Start your arm stroke by tracing the outside of an imaginary barrel in front of you. At the point then your hand, elbow and shoulder are all aligned on top of each other, then move your whole arm as a unit back quickly towards the finish of the stroke, without letting your elbow slip down.

*Figure 8: Start your arm stroke by tracing the outside of an imaginary barrel in order to keep your elbow high*

Step 5: Now try it while swimming. Make your hand

and arm feel like they are going over a barrel, then use the arm as a whole to complete the stroke by pushing back quickly to finish.

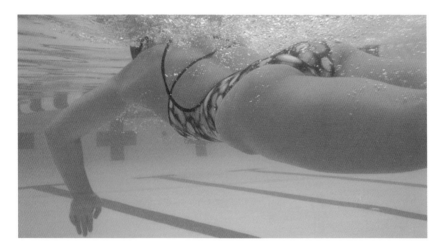

## Drill feedback chart

| PROBLEM | MODIFICATION |
| --- | --- |
| When am I supposed to feel my catch? | You should feel your hand make its catch as soon as it descends into the water. If you are having trouble feeling it, change the pitch of your hand slightly at the wrist. Experiment several times to find the ideal hand pitch for you that will allow you to catch as early as possible. |
| My elbow seems to drop down near the end of the stroke. | Practice keeping it high throughout the arm stroke. You are strongest with a high elbow, and weakest with a low elbow. |
| I feel that I am not getting the full length of my stroke in front by reaching over a barrel. | Your hand should reach to full extension before descending around the barrel. Practice this. It is important. |

## 9. ELBOW EXTENSION

### The purpose of this drill

- Feeling ideal arm stroke alignment
- Getting the maximum length of stroke
- Understanding how the elbow can affect the stroke

### How to do this drill

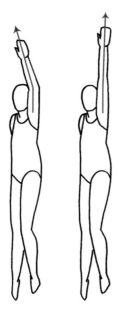

Step 1: Stand in front of a full-length mirror, arms extended above your head. Beginning with your left arm, trace the path of the freestyle arm stroke from entry to extension and catch to downsweep, upsweep through the finish near your hip. As the right arm approaches its starting point, begin to trace the path of the stroke with your left arm. Continue this for several cycles.

Step 2: After several complete arm stroke cycles, freeze one of your arms the next time it reaches the point where it would enter the water. Notice that your hand is not pointed straight ahead. Notice that your elbow is bent.

*Figure 9: Extend your elbow after entry to align your stroke forward*

Step 3: Continue watching your stroke in the mirror. Now, freeze your arm an instant later in the stroke, after you push your elbow forward, preparing to catch. Notice that now your hand is pointing straight ahead. Notice that your elbow has no bend. Notice that your hand, elbow and shoulder align forward.

Step 4: Now try it in the water. Swim freestyle for several arm cycles. Identify the different parts of the stroke as you swim: entry, extension, catch, downsweep,

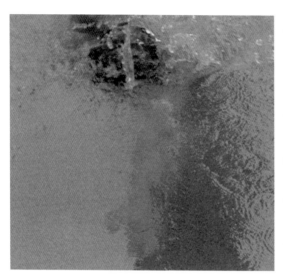

upsweep and finish. Then, freeze as your hand makes its entry. Notice the alignment of your arm. At this point in the stroke–before the extension–you hand is pointing inward, not straight ahead as it should be. Try it again, reaching to full elbow extension after the entry. Repeat, finding your extension with each stroke.

## Drill feedback chart

| PROBLEM | MODIFICATION |
|---|---|
| It feels like I lose my rhythm if I add the extension before the catch. | The extension does add another beat to the stroke. It also aligns your body forward in the water, reducing drag and allowing you to produce forward motion with less effort. |
| My elbow is not bent, but my hand aligns with my head, not with my shoulder. | Train your arm to align forward—straight up from your shoulder. Try swimming directly over the black line on the bottom of the pool. Make sure your extension brings your arm parallel to that line. |
| When I add the extension, I don't seem to be as fast. | What you might be feeling is that your stroke rate is a bit slower. That is fine. As you practice, hopefully you will feel that longer, well-aligned strokes are actually less work and more productive than shorter strokes that require a higher turnover rate. |

## **10.** 3D FREESTYLE

### The purpose of this drill

- Achieving a sweeping arm stroke
- Making the most of the water within your reach
- Learning to hold on to the water

### How to do this drill

Step 1: Before you get into the water, take a moment to think about your underwater freestyle arm stroke. Can you describe the path it takes? From the point that your hand enters the water, until the point that it exits the water, how does it travel? How can you best hold on to the water? Would it be a semi-circle? Would it be a straight line? Think about how your hand moves and describe it.

Step 2: Now, get in the water and swim several laps of freestyle. Focus on the path of your hand through the arm stroke on the horizontal plane. From the entry, it should start wide, then sweep inward under your belly button, then finally out past your hip.

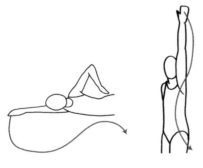

Step 3: Swim several laps of freestyle again. Focus on the path of your hand through the arm stroke on the vertical plane. From the entry, it should extend forward then descend downward to about 45 degrees until it sweeps upward back towards your body, then finally travels straight back past your hip.

Figure 10: The three dimensional path of the freestyle arm stroke

Step 4: Now, take a moment to describe the path of the underwater freestyle arm stroke again.

## Drill feedback chart

| PROBLEM | MODIFICATION |
| --- | --- |
| I seem to get more lift when I use a semi-circular underwater arm stroke. | The main purpose of the arm stroke is to move you forward, rather than to give you lift. And, the more forward motion you create, the better you will stay up. |
| So, my path should go deep to shallow, and, wide to narrow... correct? | Yes! And then the hand passes straight back past the hip. |
| I seem to lose my hold on the water when it is close to my body. | Try adjusting your wrist position so that it is pushing directly back on the water at all times. |

# 11. ACCELERATE THE ARM STROKE

## The purpose of this drill

- Learning to generate speed
- Using momentum
- Keeping hold of the water

## How to do this drill

Step 1: Swim several laps of freestyle, identifying the various stages of the underwater arm stroke as they occur in each stroke: entry, extension and catch, downsweep, upsweep, finish.

Step 2: Now, try to make each stage faster than the previous one, so at the finish of each stroke, your hand is traveling the fastest.

Step 3: In order to keep a solid hold on the water, it is necessary to accelerate the underwater arm stroke from start to finish. If your hand travels the same speed throughout, you will not be making use of the momentum you have created. Try it again. Feel your hand speed up through the path of the stroke. Feel the water in your hand as you do.

*Figure 11: Accelerate the arm stroke towards the back.*

## Drill feedback chart

| Problem | MODIFICATION |
|---|---|
| I don't know what it feels like to hold on to the water. | If you stand and sweep your hand back and forth quickly under the water, you will feel as if your hand is full of Jell-o. You should have this feeling throughout the underwater arm stroke. |
| When I push back past my hip, my hand comes out of the water. | Make sure your hand is positioned so you are pushing the water straight back with your hand, instead of lifting the water up. |
| When I think about accelerating my stroke, I forget to keep my elbow up. | Good observation. Go only as fast as you can do it correctly—that is with your elbow up. As you practice more, try adding more and more acceleration. |

## RECOVERY DRILLS

Freestyle recovery, or the part of the arm stroke that is out of the water is the only time in the stroke when your arm can rest from applying pressure to the water. It is therefore important to make the recovery as effortless as possible to save your energy for the underwater stroke. Learning to use the muscles of the core to throw your arm forward accomplishes this, as well as creating a working relationship between the two arms. Use the following drills to improve your recovery technique for freestyle.

## 12. TRAILING HAND

### The purpose of this drill

- Learning to relax the recovering arm
- Avoiding stressful shoulder rotation
- Developing an effortless recovery

### How to do this drill

Step 1: Swim freestyle for several laps. Then, focus on your right arm only. Breathe to the right so you can watch your recovery. Freeze at the point when your elbow passes your shoulder on the way to the front. Notice where your hand is. Is it in front of your elbow? Is it lined up with your elbow? Is it trailing behind your elbow?

Step 2: At the point when your elbow and your shoulder are lined up as your arm travels back to the front in the recovery, your hand should be trailing behind your shoulder and elbow. Try it again. Swim freestyle, focusing on your right arm as it recovers. Breathe to the right so you can watch it. Push your elbow forward so that your hand follows behind it.

Step 3: Swim freestyle again. Focus on your left arm as it recovers. Breathe to the left so you can watch it. Push your elbow forward so that your hand follows behind it. Your hand should be relaxed as it trails behind your elbow. Only when your hand passes your head should you throw it forward, in front of your shoulder.

Step 4: Swim freestyle again. Focus on both arms during recovery. Feel the hand of your recovering arm trailing. Feel it hanging relaxed until it passes your head and you throw it forward to start another stroke.

*Figure 12: Recover with your hand trailing behind your shoulder and elbow*

## Drill feedback chart

| PROBLEM | MODIFICATION |
| --- | --- |
| My hand leads through-out my recovery. | When you are transitioning from the underwater finish to your recovery, lift your arm out of the water elbow first... not hand first. Practice this. It is important. |
| When I try to let my hand trail, it drags through the water. | Make sure your elbow is positioned higher than your shoulder during recovery, so your trailing hand will clear the water. It should feel as if a string is attached to your elbow and someone is pulling it upward. |
| My hand stops trailing my elbow before it passes my head. | The longer you can maintain a trailing hand, the more rest, or recovery your muscles will get. |

## 13. LOOSE HAND SWING

### The purpose of this drill

* Developing an effortless recovery
* Achieving a high elbow recovery
* Aligning your recovery forward

### How to do this drill

Step 1: Float face down in the water, with your right arm extended in front of you, and your left arm at your side. You will find that you tend to float with your left shoulder higher than your right shoulder. Use the steady flutter kick to produce forward motion.

Step 2: From this position, lift your left elbow until it points straight up toward the sky, and your hand hangs down relaxed near your shoulder.

Step 3: Holding your high elbow stable, begin to swing your hand near the surface of the water, back and forth parallel to your body. Allow it to swing about twelve inches to the back and twelve inches to the front. Make sure your hand is very relaxed, both in the fingers and at the wrist. Swing your hand back and forth six times.

Step 4: Switch sides so that you are floating with your left arm extended in front of you, and your right arm is at your side. You will tend to float with your right shoulder higher than your left shoulder. Lift your right elbow until it points straight up toward the

*Figure 13: With your elbow pointing straight up, swing your loose hand back and forth*

sky, and your hand hangs down relaxed near your shoulder. With your right elbow high and stable, swing your hand back and forth near the surface of the water, parallel to the length of your body. Swing it about twelve inches in either direction. Let your hand, wrist and fingers be relaxed. Swing your hand back and forth six times.

Step 5: Repeat Steps 1 - 4 until you are able to hold your elbow steadily at a right angle to your body—pointing to the sky, and maintain a relaxed hand that swings comfortably back and forward.

## Drill feedback chart

| PROBLEM | MODIFICATION |
| --- | --- |
| How am I supposed to breathe? | You can roll to the side and catch a breath when you need it, or simply stand up, take a breath and start again. |
| It's hard to get my elbow to point to the sky. | Try rolling more on to your side, so your elbow is already positioned high. |
| It's hard to get my hand to relax. | Practice more. It should feel like you have no bones in your wrist, hand and fingers. |

# 14. POCKET

## The purpose of this drill

- Making a good transition from finish to recovery
- Beginning the recovery motion with the elbow
- Achieving a relaxed recovery

## How to do this drill

Step 1: Stand in front of a full-length mirror wearing jeans or trousers. Turn so your left side faces the mirror. Place your left hand in your left front pocket.

Step 2: Observe the motion of your left arm as you remove your hand from the pocket. What part of your arm moves first? What direction are your fingers pointing when they come out of the pocket? Try it again. Turn so your right side faces the mirror and observe your hand come out of your right front pocket. Repeat several times.

*Figure 14: Begin your recovery as if you are taking your hand out of your pocket*

Step 3: Get in the water and start swimming freestyle. As your hand reaches the end of the underwater arm stroke and prepares to transition to the recovery, imagine that you are taking it out of your pocket. Feel your elbow move first. Feel your fingers slide out of the water last. Repeat several times.

## Drill feedback chart

| PROBLEM | MODIFICATION |
|---|---|
| Should my arm be straight before I transition to the recovery? | Yes. You want to use the full extend of your arm's reach. Your hand should finish past your hip. Once your arm is straight, then do the Pocket drill. |
| I have to be rolled on to my side a bit to get my hand to clear the water when I do this drill. | That is exactly right! |
| After my hand comes out of my pocket while I am swimming... then what? | Let your elbow continue to lead your relaxed hand to the front of the stroke. |

## BREATHING DRILLS

Breathing in freestyle is a necessary part of the stroke. However, it is also the most common area that swimmers lose stroke momentum, produce drag and lose alignment. One solution is to breathe less frequently, but this is not practical in terms of accomplishing more than a few laps.

A better solution is to learn to make breathing a seamless element of the stroke that is accomplished without disrupting the momentum, form or line of the stroke. Use the following drills to improve your breathing technique for freestyle.

## **15.** REACH TO INHALE

### The purpose of this drill

- Experiencing the correct timing for breathing
- Developing breathing rhythm
- Holding alignment while breathing

### How to do this drill

Step 1: Float face down in the water, with your right arm extended in front of you, and your left arm at your side. You will find that you tend to float with your left shoulder higher than your right shoulder. Use the steady flutter kick to produce forward motion.

Step 2: Continue kicking in this position for twelve kicks, gradually exhaling through your nose and mouth. After twelve kicks, roll more to your right until your face clears the water. Inhale. Make sure that your right arm remains extended forward while you inhale. Roll back to your original position. Repeat several times.

Step 3: Try it floating with your left arm extended in front of you. Do twelve kicks while exhaling gradually, then roll more to the left so your face clears the water enough to inhale. Check that your left arm remains extended through your inhale. Roll back you your face is in the water. Repeat several times.

*Figure 15: Reach as you inhale*

Step 4: Now try incorporating this breathing position into your freestyle. Swim freestyle, breathing on your left side. When your right arm extends forward, roll to your right so your face clears the water. Reach forward while you are inhaling. As you face returns to the water, then allow your right arm to descend into the underwater stroke. Repeat several times. Try it breathing to the right.

Step 5: Time your inhale to your arm extension. Feel the long line of your body, from fingertips to toes floating on its side as you inhale. Notice that from this position you still move forward as you inhale.

## Drill feedback chart

| PROBLEM | MODIFICATION |
| --- | --- |
| It is hard to hold my breath for twelve kicks. | Use a quicker kick. Also, remember you are not holding your breath. You should be gradually exhaling, so when you finish your twelve kicks all you have to do is inhale. |
| When I am swimming, my hand sinks when I inhale. | Press your ear and temple into the water as you inhale. Actively reach forward. |
| I get it on my left side, but not my right side. | Most people have a more natural breathing side. But it is important to achieve this position on both sides to hold alignment and momentum. Practice more. |

## 16. BREATHE FROM THE HIPS

### The purpose of this drill

- Learning to roll from the hips
- Getting comfortable on your side
- Incorporating the breathing action into your stroke

### How to do this drill

Step 1: Stand facing a full-length mirror, arms at your sides. Rotate your left shoulder forward, and your right shoulder back, then switch. Continue alternating shoulders, forward and back. Notice that as you do this, your hips stay still.

Step 2: Again standing facing a full-length mirror, arms at your sides, rotate your left hip forward, and your right hip back, then switch. Continue alternating hips, forward and back. Notice that as you do this, your shoulders follow the same movement.

Step 3: In the water, float face down, arms at your sides. Without using your arms or legs, attempt to roll over to your back, initiating the roll from the shoulders. Notice that it is quite difficult to make this roll.

Step 4: Try it again. This time use your hips to initiate the roll. Notice that your shoulders follow you hips and you can easily roll to your back.

Step 5: Try it while swimming freestyle. When it is time to breathe, initiate your roll from the hips, not from the shoulders and not from the head.

*Figure 16: Initiate your inhale by rolling from the hips*

Notice that by initiating the roll to breathe from the hips that it becomes part of the regular swimming motion. Repeat several times.

## Drill feedback chart

| PROBLEM | MODIFICATION |
| --- | --- |
| Rolling like this really slows down my stroke. | It's not a bad thing to have a slower turnover, especially if you are developing efficiency. As you practice more, you can transform the roll into more of a snap, and regain some of your stroke rate. |
| There seems to be some lag time from when I roll my hips and when my shoulders and head follow. | Tighten the muscles of your core to shorten that lag time. |
| Does this mean that I don't turn my head to breathe? | In order to create the least drag possible, try to use your body's roll that is already present in the stroke, and add as little extra head roll as possible. |

## 17. CONSTANT BREATHING

### The purpose of this drill

- Learning to avoid holding your breath
- Feeling the continuous exchange of air
- Developing a breathing rhythm

### How to do this drill

Step 1: Run at medium speed once around a track. Notice that your breathing falls into a pattern of rhythmic inhaling and exhaling.

Step 2: Try it again. This time run only about 100 yards at the same speed you used the first run. Try holding your breath as you run. Only inhale and exhale when you absolutely have to. Notice that there is little rhythm to your breathing. Notice that it is not sustainable.

Step 3: Try it in the pool. Swim freestyle at medium speed for 100 yards. Hold your breath as you swim. Only inhale and exhale when you absolutely have to. Notice there is little rhythm to your breathing. Notice that it is not sustainable.

Step 4: Now try swimming freestyle at the same speed. Use a breathing rhythm of every three or four strokes. When your face is in the water, use a gradual exhale so there is a continuous stream of bubbles flowing from your nose and mouth. Just before you turn to inhale, give an extra strong puff to empty your lungs, then inhale quick and deep. Continue this rhythm for 100 yards. Could you keep going with this rhythm?

Step 5: Keep swimming with a rhythmic breathing pattern. Never break the rhythm by holding your breath.

Figure 17: Use a constant breathing rhythm, never holding your breath

## Drill feedback chart

| PROBLEM | MODIFICATION |
|---|---|
| If I exhale continuously, I am afraid I will run out of air before its time to inhale. | Practice different breathing rhythms. Every other stroke might be better for you, or every three strokes. Find the right rhythm for you. |
| I am a sprinter. Breathing rhythm isn't a big part of my events. | Even if you only breathe twice or three times during your race, learning to exhale continuously, and to inhale quick and deep is important to fuel your swimming. Also, sprinters can benefit from practicing longer distances, so it is not a waste of your time to develop rhythmic breathing skills. |
| If I hold my breath, water doesn't go up my nose. | You accomplish the same thing by exhaling through your nose by producing a gentle but continuous stream of bubbles out of your nostrils. At the same time, you are getting rid of used air, so that when you turn your head you don't have to use that short window of opportunity to expel air before you inhale. |

## LEVERAGE DRILLS

Leverage is a major part of swimming well. It works with all aspects of the stroke including floatation, kicking, arm stroke, recovery, breathing and coordination. Many of the drills you have already practiced throughout the Freestyle section of this book have made use of leverage. It is important to practice making use of leverage in the water, because it is not quite as easy as it is on land. In swimming, the swimmer must create his or her own stability to create leverage from, unlike on land where the ground itself provides stability. Use the following drills to improve your leverage in freestyle.

## 18. LEAN IN, LEAN OUT

### The purpose of this drill

- Using leverage with the arm stroke
- Powering the arm stroke with your core
- Feeling a longer, stronger arm stroke

### How to do this drill

Step 1: Begin swimming freestyle. As your left arm enters the water and extends into the catch, feel your left hip and shoulder lean left into the stroke while your left arm descends into the water.

Step 2: As your left arm prepares to do the upsweep, your left hip and shoulder begin to lean to the right and are fully leaning right while the left arm finishes the underwater stroke.

Step 3: Now focus on both of your arms. As your left arm enters the water and extends into the catch, and your left hip and shoulder are leaning into the stroke, what is happening with your right arm? Notice that while all this is happening on your left side, your right arm in transitioning to the finish of the stroke, and your right shoulder and hip are leaning out of the stroke.

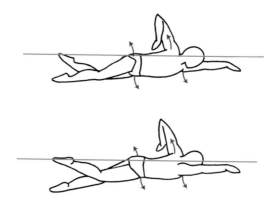

*Figure 18: Lean in and lean out of each stroke with your shoulders and hips*

otice that as you create leverage by leaning
atically create the leverage needed on the
.

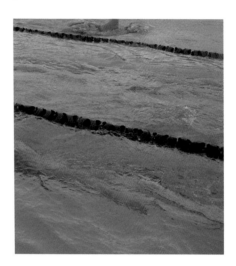

## Drill feedback chart

| PROBLEM | MODIFICATION |
| --- | --- |
| How do you know how much to lean in and out of your stroke? | You want to lean in enough to extend your reach and provide power to your descending arm. You want to lean out enough to help your hand finish fast, and clear the water easily as you start your recovery. |
| This means that the movement of my right and left arm is not independent of each other. | Exactly! It is all a unified movement. Think of your arm stroke as starting from the fingers of your left hand, and continuing through your body all the way to the fingers of your right hand. |
| Does leaning in and leaning out will improve my arm stroke timing too? | Yes, because it is an integrated part of the arm stroke leverage that works on both sides simultaneously. |

## 19. NO FLAT FREESTYLE!

### The purpose of this drill

- Feeling the importance of leverage
- Realizing the limitations of flat freestyle
- Using leverage throughout the stroke

### How to do this drill

Step 1: From a standing position, hold a tennis ball in one of your hands. Without moving your body at all, throw the ball forward overhand. Notice where it lands.

Step 2: Prepare to throw the ball again. This time as your arm moves back overhead, allow your same side shoulder and hip to move back with it. Throw the ball. Notice that it sails much farther through the air than your first throw.

Step 3: Do a similar exercise in the water. Swim freestyle. As you perform the arm stroke and flutter kick, keep your body exactly flat. Imagine you are floating on a board and that only your arms and legs are free to move. Notice that is your arm strokes are shorter. Notice that it is more difficult for your hand to clear the water as you go in to the recovery. Notice that you have less range of motion.

Figure 19: Engage your hips for more stroke length and power

Step 4: Swim freestyle again. As you hand passes your head moving to the front in the recovery, engage your same side hip and shoulder to drive your arm forward for the entry, extension and catch. As you hand prepares to move from the downsweep to the upsweep phase, engage your opposite hip and shoulder to send leverage to the finish of your arm stroke. Notice that each arm stroke is longer. Notice that each arm stroke carries more power. Notice that you are using leverage.

## Drill feedback chart

| PROBLEM | MODIFICATION |
| --- | --- |
| I feel more in control when I swim flat. | At first it is unsettling to float any way other than flat in the water. But through practice you can become comfortable changing your floating position to lean in and out of your stroke. You control to what extent you lean in and lean out, and you control the amount of leverage produced. |
| I am able to lean in well, but not so good at leaning out. | For most people it is easier to lean in to their stroke with their shoulder and hip, by rolling them downward. It is not so easy to roll them upward. So, focus instead at that point on leaning into the stroke with the opposite side shoulder and hip. By doing so, the hip and shoulder that should lean out will do so automatically. |
| Doesn't leaning in and out of your stroke create more drag han swimming flat? | Good point. There has to be a very good reason to create drag. In this case that good reason is to make use of leverage that provides a great deal of power to the stroke. |

## **20.** MAINTAIN THE CENTERLINE

### The purpose of this drill

- Holding your alignment
- Maintaining a stable axis
- Using your fulcrum

### How to do this drill

Step 1: Stick a long piece of masking tape in the middle of a full-length mirror from the floor to about your height. Now stick another piece of masking tape vertically down the center of your body, starting at your chin. This is your centerline, and you want it to remain straight at all times. Your centerline works as both your axis for alignment, and your fulcrum to make leverage possible.

Step 2: Stand in front of the taped mirror. Line up the tape on the mirror with the tape on your centerline. With your arms at your sides, start swinging your hips and shoulders forward and backward, about the same amount that you do when you lean in and out of your stroke. Use the same rate as your stroke rate. Check to see if the tape on the mirror and the tape marking your centerline stay lined up. If so, you are maintaining alignment.

Step 3: Now simulate your freestyle stroke as you stand in front of the mirror. Make sure to include the arm entry, extension and catch, down and upsweep, and the fast finish. Make sure to include the roll that produces leverage for each stroke. Repeat for several stroke cycles. Check to see if the tape on the mirror and the tape marking your centerline stay lined up. If so, you are staying on your axis.

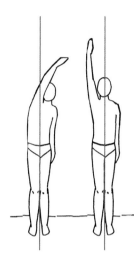

Step 4: Try it in the water. In this case, you have to imagine your centerline. Use the line on the bottom of the pool as you did the tape on the mirror. Swim freestyle. Entry, extension and catch, down and upsweep, and fast finish. Roll in and roll out to gain leverage. Check to see if your centerline is lined up with the line on the bottom of the pool. Are you maintaining your alignment and axis? Is your centerline fulcrum producing leverage for you? Repeat.

*Figure 20: Stay aligned with your centerline*

## Drill feedback chart

| PROBLEM | MODIFICATION |
| --- | --- |
| The centerline of my hips is always moving! | Make sure you are rolling your hips, that is turning one forward while the other goes back, as opposed to wagging your hips where both hips move to the right and then to the left. This is an important distinction. |
| When I am "swimming" in the mirror at the point that my arm is fully extended, my centerline is sorted of bowed outward at the hip. | This could mean that your hip is compensating for your extended arm being out of alignment. Check to see if your extended hand is aligned with your shoulder as it should be, or if it is over-reaching to the middle. |
| I am not sure if I feel the fulcrum. | Think of the titter-totter. One side goes up and the other goes down, but what it is balancing on stays still and stable throughout this movement. What you are balancing on while swimming is your centerline, which if kept stable and centered, works as a fulcrum. |

## 21. THE KICK LEVER

### The purpose of this drill

- Connecting the kick and the arm stroke
- Finding leverage between the arms and the legs
- Timing the kick to the arm stroke

### How to do this drill

Step 1: Swim freestyle using a 2-beat kick—that is one kick with each arm stroke during a complete stroke cycle. Time the downbeat of your kick so it happens as you make your catch with the opposite side hand. Practice until you are able to maintain this timing easily. Notice that the power from downbeat of the kick travels up and across your body improving the quality of your catch. Try it again. As you kick down, feel the water in your hand.

Step 2: Now swim freestyle with a 4-beat kick—that is two kicks with each arm stroke during a complete stroke cycle. Time the downbeat of the first kick so it happens as you make your catch with the opposite side hand. Time the downbeat of the second kick so it happens as you transition to the finish phase of the same side arm stroke. Practice until you are able to maintain this complicated timing easily. Feel the first kick assist your catch. Feel the second kick help you achieve a fast finish of your arm stroke.

*Figure 21: Time the downbeat of your kick so it happens as you make your catch with the opposite hand*

Step 3: Now swim freestyle with a 6-beat kick—that is three kicks with each arm stroke during a complete stroke cycle. Time the downbeat of the first kick so it happens as you make your catch with the opposite side hand. Time the downbeat of the second kick or third so it happens as you transition to the finish phase of the same side arm stroke. Practice until it feels natural. Feel your hand make a solid catch. Feel your hand finish fast.

## Drill feedback chart

| PROBLEM | MODIFICATION |
|---|---|
| I can't get the timing. | It is complicated, especially at the 4-beat kick stage. Try focusing on only the kick/catch lever in your stroke at first. Practice this for a long time, then add in the kick/finish lever. When you proceed to the 6-beat stage, it is actually easier to match the kicks to these points in your arm stroke, because there are more available kicks. |
| Why do a 6-beat kick if there are only four points that produce leverage? | The main purpose of the kick is to produce forward motion, so the more kicks the better. Gaining leverage in this way is a bonus. |
| It seems that as well as helping my catch, the first kick helps me roll into my stroke. | Excellent! Use this discovery to your advantage. |

## COORDINATION DRILLS

Developing a great freestyle requires becoming skilled at numerous elements of the stroke. However without the ability to coordinate these many individual parts into one seamless effort, great freestyle will remain elusive. It is useful to look at each individual part of the stroke as having multiple purposes, like links in a chain, they connect not to one other link, but to two. Coordinating freestyle is a matter of sequencing and timing the many parts of the stroke so they benefit each other, and the stroke as a whole. Use the following drills to improve your coordination in freestyle.

## **22.** UNITED STROKES

### The purpose of this drill

- Feeling the connection between the arms
- Using your core to connect your stroke
- Feeling one stroke action initiate another

### How to do this drill

Step 1: Swim freestyle for several laps. Emphasize stroke rhythm. Emphasize leverage. Emphasize quality in each element of the stroke.

Step 2: Swim twelve stroke cycles, then freeze as your left arm is entering the water. Notice what your right arm is doing at this point in the stroke. Notice how your body is leaning into one side and out of the other side simultaneously. Notice how your core is affecting each arm differently at the same time.

Step 3: Swim twelve more stroke cycles, then freeze as your left arm is transitioning into the finish. Notice what your right arm is doing at this point in the stroke. Notice how your body is leaning into one side and out of the other side simultaneously. Notice how your core is affecting each arm differently at the same time.

Step 4: Swim twelve more stroke cycles, then freeze as your left arm moves into its recovery. Notice what your right arm is doing at this point in the stroke. Notice how your body is leaning into

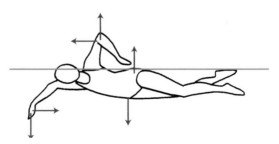

*Figure 22: Leverage from the core simultaneously affects each side differently*

one side and out of the other side simultaneously. Notice how your core is affecting each arm differently at the same time.

Step 5: Practice until you feel that your arm stroke has become one single united stroke extending from left hand to right hand with your core, or Power Zone in the middle.

Drill feedback chart

| PROBLEM | MODIFICATION |
|---------|--------------|
| I'm not sure I feel the connection. | When one arm is high, the other arm is low. When one arm is reaching to the front the other arm is pushing to the back. Your core connects these efforts and while it powers one side, it simultaneously stabilizes the other. Practice more. |
| Does this mean the arms should be exactly opposite? | There are times in the stroke when the arms are opposite, but there are also times when they are not. This happens because the stroke changes speed throughout. There are points when one arm catches up to the other. Still, each arm is performing a different function, and your core is assisting both at the same time. |
| So, if I understand this correctly, there is no time when the arms move unassisted by the core. | Correct! Freestyle is driven from your core, as if you were paddling a kayak. Both arms are doing their part, neither of which would work well alone. Both arms are powered by the muscles of the core simultaneously, as the body leans in and out of the paddling motion. |

## 23. REACH AND RECOVER

### The purpose of this drill

- Feeling the relationship between the extension and the recovery
- Powering two different actions at the same time
- Feeling power from the core

### How to do this drill

Step 1: Standing in chest deep water, bend forward at the waist and perform the freestyle arm stroke, including breathing.

Step 2: After several strokes, freeze when your left arm is at full extension in front. Notice that your body is leaning into that extension, so that the left shoulder lower than the right, providing leverage to the beginning of the arm stroke. At the same time, the right arm should be in mid recovery. Notice that the right side of the body is leaning out, so that the right shoulder is higher than the left, allowing the recovering arm to clear the water.

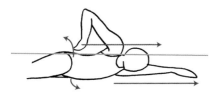

*Figure 23: Reach as you recover with the other arm*

Step 3: Now swim several laps of freestyle. Focus on your left side only. Notice the pitch of your body toward your left arm as it extends. Feel the power flow up from your core and drive your extension farther. After focusing on your left side only for several laps, notice that without consciously making it happen, at the same time, the right side of your body is pitched upward perfectly to perform the recovery. Repeat several times.

## Drill feedback chart

| PROBLEM | MODIFICATION |
| --- | --- |
| When my right arm is recovering, my left arm is pulling deep underwater. | Try to focus on the entry, extension and catch. These three elements need to happen high in the water, before your hand descends. Practice spending more time reaching towards the other end of the pool before allowing your arm to descend. Otherwise you will miss out on the available leverage for the catch when your left side is low. |
| When I am extending with my left arm, my right arm is just starting the recovery. | Try to accelerate your finish so you can start your recovery sooner. Otherwise you will miss the window of opportunity when your right side is at its highest to recover with the least amount of effort. |
| So I can achieve leverage for both arms only concentrating on one? | Yes! As long as your stroke timing is correct, your core will drive both sides simultaneously. |

## 24. CATCH AND PUSH

### The purpose of this drill

- Feeling the relationship between the catch and the finish
- Powering two different actions at the same time
- Feeling power from the core

### How to do this drill

Step 1: Standing in chest deep water, bend forward at the waist and perform the freestyle arm stroke, including breathing.

Step 2: After several strokes, freeze when your left arm is making its catch in front. Notice that your body is pitched down into that catch, so that the left shoulder lower than the right, providing leverage to that action. At the same time, the right arm should be accelerating to the finish of the stroke. Notice that the right side of the body is pitched upward, so that the right shoulder is higher than the left, assisting with the speed of the finish.

Step 3: Now swim several laps of freestyle. Focus on your left side only. Notice that your body is moving downward on your left side as that hand makes its catch. Feel the power flow up from your core and give your catching hand a solid grip on the water. After focusing on your left side only for several laps, notice that without consciously making it happen, at the same time, the right side of your body is moving upward adding power to the fast finish. Repeat several times.

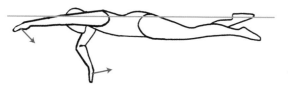

*Figure 24: Catch with one hand as you transition from pull to push with the other.*

## Drill feedback chart

| PROBLEM | MODIFICATION |
| --- | --- |
| When my left hand is catching water, my right hand is already recovering. | Make sure you are maintaining a high elbow throughout your underwater arm stroke so your hand is not just slipping through the water too quickly without producing forward motion. Focus on making the most of the downsweep, upsweep and finish and this timing issue should resolve. |
| When my left arm is catching water, my right arm has not started the finish. | Your downsweep may be to long or too slow. You might need sweep upward sooner, or start accelerating your stroke earlier. Remember that each phase gets faster, beginning with the entry, extension and catch, through the downsweep and upsweep, to the finish. |
| So at the beginning of these actions, my arms are not opposite, but by the end of it they are, correct? | Yes! Because the finish is such a quick motion, your hand travels a significant distance while the catching hand is stays in front near the surface in order to fully engage the water. |

## **25.** SWIMMING TALL

### The purpose of this drill

- Maintaining length of stroke
- Having a reaching arm at all times
- Eliminating drag

### How to do this drill

Step 1: Swim several laps of freestyle at a comfortable pace. Focus on utilizing available leverage by rolling into and out of your stroke. Focus on connecting the movements on either side of your body. Focus on driving your stroke from the core.

Step 2: With each stroke make the most of the extension in front. Coordinate your stroke so that at the point when one arm is extending, the other is recovering. Observe that at this point in the stroke neither arm is actively engaged in producing forward motion. Notice that despite this fact, your body is still moving forward.

Step 3: Continue to swim freestyle, focusing on that point when one arm is extending and the other is out of the water recovering. How is it that the body continues to move forward without any effort from your upper body? This is the most streamlined position of the freestyle stroke. It produces the least drag and makes the most of the momentum of the previous stroke. This is your tall position, and it is your secret weapon.

Step 4: Continue to swim freestyle. When your reaching arm leaves the front, quickly replace it with the other arm so there is always one arm reaching. Think tall. Swim tall. Do it all the time.

*Figure 25: Make the most of the extension in the front of the arm stroke to be streamlined and swim tall*

## Drill feedback chart

| PROBLEM | MODIFICATION |
|---|---|
| I feel that my momentum stops at this point in the stroke. | Make sure you are leaning into your extension, and not floating flat. |
| My extending arm sinks. | Imagine you are trying to touch the far end of the pool with each stroke. |
| There is a short time when neither of my arms is reaching. | Work on eliminating this time. You want to be tall at all times. the taller you swim, the more advantage you have. While there is no reaching happening, you miss out on this. |

## DRILLS FOR BACKSTROKE

## BODY POSITION DRILLS

Good body position in backstroke is often misunderstood. From the time we were in swim lessons as young children many of us heard, "Push your tummy up!" And when we did that, sure enough, our face went into the water upside down leaving us with such a memorable experience of water filled sinuses that we decided that backstroke was an awful stroke, and we have avoided it as much as possible ever since. So, let's take time to relearn the basic backstroke float, to ensure it is comfortable and stable and maybe even something we might enjoy! Use the following drills to improve your body position in backstroke.

## 26. SPINE LINE

### The purpose of this drill

- Floating comfortably on your back
- Floating well on your back
- Using core tension to achieve a good backstroke position

### How to do this drill

Step 1: Lay face up on the pool deck. Relax your neck and shoulders. Press your spine into the ground from the back of your neck, between your shoulder blades, and even at the small of your back. Make your whole spine come in contact with the pool deck.

Step 2: Notice that this is easier to achieve with some parts of your spine, including between your shoulder blades. For other parts it is quite a challenge. To get the back of your neck to touch the pool deck you will have to pull your chin inward toward the back of your throat. To get the small of your back to touch the pool deck you will have to rotate your pelvis forward and contract your abdominal muscles. Hold this position in order to commit it to memory so you will be able to recreate it when you get in the water.

Step 3: Get in chest-deep water. With your arms extended to the sides from your shoulders, prepare to recreate the position you were in on your back on the pool deck. First, lower your shoulders into the water and lean back until your head is in the water, and the water is covering your ears. Next, allow your neck, shoulders and chest to relax as they follow your head into a horizontal position at the surface of the water.

Step 4: Now, rotate your pelvis forward, as you did on the pool deck. Engage your abdominal muscles in this action, and contract them as you gently push away from

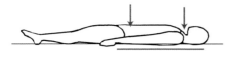

*Figure 26: Achieve a straight spine line to float upon*

the bottom of the pool with your feet. Relax. Focus on your straight spine as you float comfortably on your back.

## Drill feedback chart

| PROBLEM | MODIFICATION |
|---|---|
| I sink almost immediately. | Try again. Focus on achieving a straight spine to float upon. Make sure your pelvis is rotated forward, and that your abs are tight so your hips are high in the water. Make sure your neck and shoulders are relaxed and that your ears are underwater. If you are still having trouble, take a large breath and hold it as your feet push gently off the bottom of the pool. |
| My feet sink. | That is okay at this point. If it makes you more comfortable you can add a gentle kick to keep your legs afloat, but don't let go of your spine line or core tension. |
| I am floating high in the water with my hips and shoulders, but low in the water around my belly. | Perfect! This is the ideal backstroke floating position. |

## **27.** HEAD ON A PILLOW

### The purpose of this drill

- Developing good head position
- Achieving a relaxed neck and upper body
- Associating backstroke with comfort

### How to do this drill

Step 1: Lay down on your back with your head on your favorite pillow. Feel your head sink gently into the softness. Feel your neck and shoulders relax. Feel that no muscles are engaged because your head is supported by your wonderful pillow.

Step 2: Keeping your pillow in mind, get into chest deep water. Lower your shoulders into the water. Gently lay the back of your head back so the water surrounds your face at the hairline. Allow your neck, shoulders and chest to follow. Relax your arms as they float extended out from your shoulders. Rotate your pelvis forward and engage your abdominal muscles. Give a gentle push off the bottom of the pool with your feet and float on your spine.

Step 3: Focus on your head as it floats comfortably in the water, as if it is being supported by your favorite pillow. Repeat several times until you achieve a fully relaxed head and neck while floating on your back.

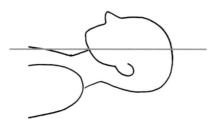

*Figure 27: Let your head float relaxed as if it was resting on a pillow*

## Drill feedback chart

| PROBLEM | MODIFICATION |
| --- | --- |
| I can't relax when water goes in my ears. | Earplugs solve this problem for many swimmers. |
| I keep worrying that the water will go over my face. | As a swimmer, you already know how to respond when your face is underwater. If the water happens to splash over your face, respond the same way: simply exhale through you nose. You can overcome this! Relax. |
| My neck is still tense. | Lower your chin. Press the back of your head and neck gently into the water. Avoid shrugging up your shoulders. Let them be low and relaxed. |

## 28. BANANA

### The purpose of this drill

- Feeling an ideal backstroke floating position
- Becoming comfortable with back float
- Gaining confidence for backstroke

### How to do this drill

Step 1: Float on your back with your arms at your sides. Find your spine line and balance on it, rotating your pelvis forward and engaging your abdominal muscles. Relax your neck.

Step 2: Focus on your abs. Are they holding your pelvis in a forward position so your spine is straight at the small of your back? Contract your abdominal muscles more so that your pelvis and your chest move slightly closer together.

Step 3: You should be floating in a high chest and high feet position. Your belly button should be underwater, lower than your chest and feet. From the side, your body should resemble the shape of a banana. Try it again.

*Figure 28: Float with high hips and high shoulders while your belly button is underwater*

## Drill feedback chart

| PROBLEM | MODIFICATION |
|---------|--------------|
| I can't seem to rotate my pelvis forward very well. | Practice pulling your belly button back towards your spine as you push your hips simultaneously forward and upward. |
| I sink pretty quickly in this position. | It will take practice and a lot of abdominal strength to hold this floating position. Practice more. |
| This is exactly opposite of the way I learned to float on my back. | Yes, this is true for many swimmers, but you will find that this position sets up a much more streamlined and stable backstroke position with a far greater potential for leverage from the core. |

## KICK DRILLS

Good backstroke kickers find it a comfortable and efficient way to move through the water. These swimmers have discovered that the secret to a great backstroke kick is in the ankle. There is less range of motion by the leg in the back flutter kick than in front flutter kick, as the back flutter kick is performed almost exclusively below the bodyline. However the feet flex and rotate more in backstroke kick. In addition good backstroke kickers use as little abduction at the knee as possible to avoid producing drag. Use the following drills to improve your kicking technique for backstroke.

## 29. KICK UP!

### The purpose of this drill

- Learning to kick productively on the back
- Feeling the power phase of the backstroke kick
- Developing foot speed

### How to do this drill

Step 1 In the water, float on your back with your arms at your sides. Float on your spine in the banana position. Begin kicking using an alternating leg motion as in freestyle, but on your back.

Step 2 Begin by dropping your heel down gently into the water about twelve to fifteen inches below the surface. Then push the water up sharply using the top of your foot.

Step 3 Done correctly this kick will produce a reaction that resembles boiling water on this surface of the water. Try it again. Allow your heel to drop down below the surface of the water then kick upward with a quick short burst of force. As one foot kicks up, the other drops down.

Step 4 Keep practicing until you can produce good forward motion and a consistent boil at the surface around your feet.

Figure 29: Drop your heal down then push the water up sharply, making it boil

## Drill feedback chart

| PROBLEM | MODIFICATION |
|---|---|
| The arches of my feet are cramping. | This is common at first. There is a lot of pressure on top of the feet as they push the water up. Unlike in flutter kick with freestyle, you are kicking against gravity. Do as much as you can and adjust gradually. |
| I am not moving forward. | Make sure there is a distinct difference in force between the force you use to drop your heel into the water, and the force you use to kick up. There should be much more force in the upward kick—the power phase, and much less force in the heal drop—the recovery phase. If the force is equal, it will cancel each other out and you will not move forward. |
| Problem: I can't get the water to boil when I kick up. | Modification: Imagine there is a ball floating on he surface of the water over your feet. Without letting any part of your foot break the surface of the water, you must make the ball move into the air at least one inch. Concentrate your kick upward into a short powerful burst. Practice more. |

## 30. NO KNEES/NO TOES

### The purpose of this drill

- Eliminating potential drag
- Achieving a streamlined kick
- Feeling a productive backstroke kick

### How to do this drill

Step 1: Stand facing a wall, close enough that your toes touch the wall. Balance on your right foot. Draw your left leg back so your foot ends up about twelve to fifteen inches behind you.

Step 2: With your toes pointed, quickly sweep your foot forward so it stops exactly at the starting position. Try it again. Control the movement so neither your foot, nor your knee comes in contact with the wall in front of you. Try it several more times.

Step 3: Switch legs. Balancing on your left leg, draw your right leg back behind you so your foot moves about twelve to fifteen inches back. Point your toes and use a short, sharp kick forward to bring your foot back to the starting point. Do not pass the starting point. Avoid hitting the wall with your foot or your knee. Repeat several times.

Step 4: Try it in the water. Float on your back with your arms at your sides. Allow your left heel to drop down into the water about twelve to fifteen inches. With your toes pointed, move your foot quickly back to the starting point, put not past it. There should be no sign of your knee or your toes breaking the surface of the water. Try it several times with your left foot, then switch to your right foot.

Step 5: Now, floating on your back with your arms at your sides, try kicking regular back flutter kick using the technique you have just practiced. Your kick is limited to a space between the surface of the water and twelve to fifteen inches below the surface. You cannot break the water's surface with your toes or your knees. Kick at a rate fast enough to produce forward motion.

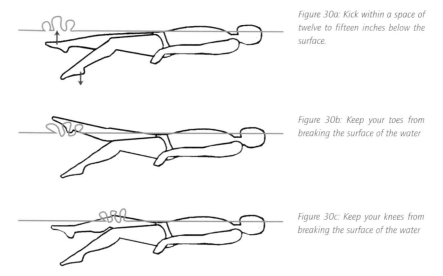

*Figure 30a: Kick within a space of twelve to fifteen inches below the surface.*

*Figure 30b: Keep your toes from breaking the surface of the water*

*Figure 30c: Keep your knees from breaking the surface of the water*

Drill feedback chart

| PROBLEM | MODIFICATION |
|---------|--------------|
| My knees keep breaking the surface. | Go back to the land part of the drill so you can watch your knees. Remember, the entire backstroke kick happens behind you. It is difficult to get used to not raising your knee because this is part of many common actions we do with our legs including walking, running, bicycling and kicking a ball. However in backstroke kick, raising the knee creates a great deal of drag and compromises the power of the kick so it is important to learn to kick without doing it. |
| My toes come out of the water. | Make sure your toes are pointed. If possible point your toes so there is a straight line from your toes to your knee. You need to create as large a surface as possible with the top of your foot with which to push the water up without breaking the surface. |
| My feet are not breaking the surface, but the water is still moving when I kick up. | Good! This means you are producing a strong kick in the power phase, and are controlling it well. The water that is moving above your feet is caused by the force of your kick displacing water as it moves upward quickly. Try to make this water boil. |

# 31. STREAMLINE BACK KICK

## The purpose of this drill

- Kicking well in a streamlined position
- Eliminating drag
- Developing foot speed

## How to do this drill

Step 1: Place your arms over your head. Clasp one hand over the other forming a point. Squeeze your ears between your arms. Lower your shoulders into the water and lean back into a floating position. Find your spine line. Relax your neck. Find the banana position.

Step 2: Start kicking flutter kick at a rate that produces enough forward motion, so that you can feel the water flow past your face. Focus on your knees. Keep them under the surface of the water. Avoid raising them at all as a part of your kick.

Step 3: Focus on your feet. Make sure your kick is contained to twelve to fifteen inches of water depth, that your toes are pointed, and that your foot does not break the surface, but makes the water boil.

Step 4: Kick at a faster rate. Feel the benefit of this streamlined position. Challenge yourself to kick faster than you are used to while holding on to the no toes/no knees technique.

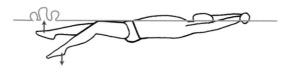

*Figure 31: Streamline backstroke kick*

Drill feedback chart

| PROBLEM | MODIFICATION |
| --- | --- |
| I kick better on my back with my arms at my sides. | It is certainly easier, but try to challenge yourself because backstroke kick in the streamline position resembles the body position used with the whole stroke quite closely. |
| I find myself arching my back in the streamlined position. | Focus on your spine line and banana position. Good body position is the foundation of good swimming. |
| I am not able to produce forward motion. | Use more force on your kick upward. Bring your foot right to the surface in a quick burst. Make sure your knees are not breaking the surface and creating drag that slows you down. Practice more. |

## **32.** THE ANKLE DRILL

### The purpose of this drill

- Making use of ankle flexibility
- Achieving pointed toes from the ankle
- Learning to relax the ankle

### How to do this drill

Step 1: Take your shoes off and lie down face up on the pool deck. Raise your legs to 90 degrees. Place your hands under your hips for stability. Focus on your ankles. Rotate your feet in outward circles ten times from the ankles. Rotate them in inward circles ten times from the ankles. Notice that your ankles have quite a range of motion.

Figure 32: Point your toes using your ankles.. Achieve a straight line from your knees to toes when you kick up.

Step 2: Now, focusing on your feet and ankles, kick flutter kick rapidly in the air using a kick that spans about twelve to fifteen inches. Imagine that you have no bones in your foot or ankle. Kick for one minute. Your feet should feel floppy. Your feel should look floppy. Repeat.

Step 3: Now, focus on your toes, feet and ankles. Using the flexibility in your ankles, make your toes go to a point. Avoid engaging your toes to achieve this position. Let them be loose. Can you achieve a straight line from your knee to your toes? Repeat.

Step 4: Get in the water and stand with your back against the wall. Hold on to the side of the pool with both arms extended to give you stability. Bring your legs up to 90 degrees and begin to kick flutter kick. Kick at a fast rate. Watch your kick. Point your toes using your ankles. Let your feet be floppy as if they had no bones. Push the water up quickly and feel it press against the top of your foot. Make the water boil.

## Drill feedback chart

| PROBLEM | MODIFICATION |
| --- | --- |
| I can't get a straight line from my knees to my toes when I point my toes. | Try rotating your feet inward closer together so the big toe on each foot nearly touches. |
| My toes are not relaxed when I point them. | It could be that you are using the arch of your foot to point your toes, rather than your ankle. Practice rotating your foot from the ankle to the pointed position, then your toes will remain relaxed. |
| When I am kicking downward, there is not a straight line from my knee to my toes. | That is fine. During the downward or recovery motion, if your foot is floppy as it should be, the water will push it up out of the toe point position. It is just during the upward kick that is must be pointed fully to involve the whole top of your foot which is your kicking surface during the power phase. |

## **33.** GOOD KNEE, BAD KNEE

### The purpose of this drill

- Understanding two kinds of knee bend
- Avoiding abduction at the hip
- Feeling the right kind of knee bend

### How to do this drill

Step 1: In shallow water, stand with your back against the side of the pool. Hold on to the side of the pool with your arms extended for stability. Raise your left leg up to 90 degrees, so it is extended in front of you at the surface of the water.

Step 2: Bring your knee closer to your chest by folding slightly inward at the hip. Is your knee bent? This is the kind of knee bend we want to avoid in backstroke. Notice that the knee breaks the surface of the water, and would be a source of drag. Notice that while you're with your knee bent this way, your whole leg is not positioned to kick, so you would lose power from the kick. Remember this as a bad knee bend.

Step 3: Return your leg to the starting position extended in front of you at the surface of the water, 90 degrees to your body. Now, drop your heal to about fifteen inches under the surface of water. Is your knee bent? This is the helpful kind of knee bend for backstroke. Notice that your knee does not break the surface of the water. Notice that with your knee bent this way that your foot is positioned well to push the water upward with force. Remember this as a good knee bend.

Step 4: Now, with your arms extended over your head in a streamline position, perform the backstroke kick. First, try a half lap with the bad knee bend. Notice that forward motion is hard to achieve. Now, kick the rest of the way with the good knee bend. Feel yourself excel with an effective backstroke kick.

*Figure 33a: A good knee bend occurs when you drop your heal*

*Figure 33b: A bad knee bend occurs when you raise your knee*

## Drill feedback chart

| PROBLEM | MODIFICATION |
|---|---|
| Does this mean that the backstroke kick uses only the leg from the knee down? | No, the power of the backstroke kick comes from the upper leg. But, by dropping the heal during the recovery, the swimmer can produce more power and less drag within the same space that would be used by a straight leg during the power phase. |
| My knees still break the surface a bit when my foot is kicking up. | Try inwardly rotating your feet. This might make all the difference. |
| It is hard not to fold at the hip when I kick. | Yes, we as humans are used to using this motion for many everyday actions including walking, running and climbing stairs. But, for an effective backstroke kick we must avoid it. Practice isolating the movement of dropping the heel while keeping everything from the knee up still. Then kick up with your whole leg. |

## ARM STROKE DRILLS

It is hard not to think of the backstroke arm stroke as following a completely circular path. After all, when we watch backstroke that is what we see happening on top of the water. But in fact what happens underwater is completely different. The hands sweep down and up in an exaggerated pull/push pattern that resembles an exaggerated Z. In many ways the backstroke arm stroke is similar to freestyle except in backstroke the whole underwater path is at the side of the body rather than under it. Use the following drills to improve your arm stroke technique for backstroke.

## **34.** Z PULL

### The purpose of this drill

- Learning the path of the backstroke arm stroke
- Feeling the deep and shallow sweep of the backstroke arms
- Maintaining a high elbow position

### How to do this drill

Step 1: Float on your back in the water with your right arm at your side and your left arm extended above your head. Feel your body lean toward with left. Begin kicking. Use your right arm only to swim the backstroke.

Step 2: Allow your left hand to travel below the surface of the water about 15 inches. Then, holding your elbow in a stable, high position, sweep your hand up and past your shoulder following a semi-circular path to your hip. Repeat several times, then switch arms.

*Figure 34: The path of the backstroke arms*

Step 3: Do it again. Feel your hand make a hair-pin turn from its deepest point after the entry as it begins its semi-circle sweep up and past the shoulder. Feel your forearm and hand pivot around your stable elbow as your arm travels toward the hip. Feel your arm achieve a 90-degree angle as it lines up with the shoulder about half way through the underwater stroke. Feel your hand travel the path of a Z. Practice more.

## Drill feedback chart

| PROBLEM | MODIFICATION |
| --- | --- |
| It seems easier to use a circular arm stroke. | It certainly is easier to learn, as it is a mirror image of the recovery. However, as your hand gets farther and farther from your body in the middle of the stroke, the weaker it gets. In addition, during the last half of the stroke, when a swimmer achieves the most effective force, by using this circular path, the hand would be traveling upward at this point, which hydro-dynamically would drive the swimmer downward in the water, not forward. |
| I don't feel the semi-circle part of the stroke. | Your elbow must be still for you to feel it. Only your fore-arm and hand are moving at that point. Think of your elbow like the hinge of a door as it is swinging. |
| My hand stays very close to my body throughout the stroke. Is that correct? | Your hand should form a right angle midway through the stroke. At that point, your elbow will be closer to your body than your hand. As you approach the end of the arm stroke, your hand will pass close to your hip. |

## **35.** DESCEND TO CATCH

### The purpose of this drill

- Finding the backstroke catch
- Feeling the backstroke catch
- Learning to catch deep

### How to do this drill

Step 1: Float on your back in the water with your right arm at your side and your left arm extended above your head. Begin kicking. Use your right arm only to swim the backstroke.

Step 2: Descend your left arm about fifteen inches into the water, using your pinkie to cut the water and lead your hand downward. Feel your left shoulder and hip also descend. Feel your right shoulder and hip rise.

Step 3: When your hand reaches its deepest point, rotate your palm outward and make your catch. As you start to sweep your hand up and past your shoulder in a semi-circular motion, feel the pressure of the water against your hand and forearm. Repeat several times. Try it with your right arm moving.

Step 4: Now swim backstroke with two arms. Find your catch on each side.

*Figure 35: Descend your hand about fifteen inches into the water, leading with your pinkie*

## Drill feedback chart

| PROBLEM | MODIFICATION |
|---|---|
| I don't feel the catch. | Make sure your hand does not stop at its deepest point but uses the momentum of its descent to take hold of the water and vault your body forward. At its deepest point, use your wrist to turn your hand so it can press against the water. |
| I can't seem to get my hand to go very deep at the beginning of the stroke. | Lean your shoulder and hip towards the moving arm at entry to achieve more depth with your hand. |
| I enter the water with the back of my hand. | By turning your hand so your pinkie enters first, you create a smaller hole in the water, and therefore less drag. |

# 36. SHORT PULL, LONG PUSH

## The purpose of this drill

- Feeling both pull and push motions
- Making the transition from pull to push
- Holding on to the water

## How to do this drill

Step 1: Swim backstroke. Descend to your hand into the water. At its deepest point rotate your palm out and grab a hand full of water. Sweep your hand up and over your shoulder and down past your hip. Practice for several laps. Notice the point in your stroke when your hand, elbow and shoulder all line up.

Step 2: Continue swimming backstroke. After the catch of each stroke, use your hand and forearm to pull the water up into the semi-circular sweep past your shoulder, keeping your elbow high and stable. Notice that it is at the top of this semicircle that your hand, elbow and shoulder all line up.

Step 3: Continue swimming backstroke. Descend, catch and pull to the point that your hand, elbow and shoulder line up. Then, push the water through the end of the semi-circle past your shoulder and toward your hips. Notice the transition from pull to push.

Step 4: Practice again saying to yourself, "Descend, catch, pull, push." Notice that in backstroke the pull is quite short, whereas the push is very long.

*Figure 36: Pull up to the shoulder, Push past the hip.*

## Drill feedback chart

| PROBLEM | MODIFICATION: |
| --- | --- |
| I feel the pull, but not the push. | Make sure your hand, elbow and shoulder are lined up as you transition to the push. If your elbow drops and leads the way, you will not get a good push. |
| I feel the push, but not the pull. | It could be that you are not making a solid catch before your pull. Practice catching at the deepest point. Also, make sure that your elbow is stable when you start your pull. If it moves then you sacrifice this portion of your stroke. |
| I don't feel a long push. | Make sure the path of your hand travels past your shoulder and along side, rather than into your hip. The hand actually finishes the push below the hip with the hand facing the bottom of the pool. |

# 37. THROW IT!

## The purpose of this drill

- Accelerating the arm stroke
- Feeling a fast push
- Holding on to the water

## How to do this drill

Step 1: Holding a tennis ball in your left hand, lay down on the pool deck, at the edge of the pool, with the length of your body parallel to the pool edge, and your left shoulder extending over the edge.

Step 2: Extend your left arm over your head, as you would in backstroke. Without raising your hand above the level of the pool deck, throw the ball parallel to your body past your feet. Make the ball sail about 25 feet by using your arm rather than your wrist for power. Do it again. Notice the bend in your elbow about midway through the throw. Notice the point when your hand elbow and shoulder all line up.

Step 3: Prepare to throw the ball again. Position your arm extended above your head. Focus on making the flight of the ball travel about 25 feet parallel to your body. Focus on making sure your hand does not pass above the top of the pool deck.

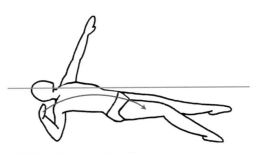

Throw it! Feel the acceleration in your hand as you send the ball into flight. Feel the ball leave your hand when it is moving at is fastest, towards the end of the throw.

*Figure 37: Throw the water past your feet*

Step 4. Get in the pool and swim backstroke using the exercise you just did. After you catch water, throw it past your feet. Throw it in a line parallel to your body. Feel your hand accelerate. Feel its fastest speed towards the end of the push. Practice more. Throw the water with every arm stroke.

## Drill feedback chart

| PROBLEM | MODIFICATION |
| --- | --- |
| I can't get the ball to go 25 feet. | Throw the ball as far as you can and focus on the acceleration of your hand. This is the point of the drill. Also, make sure you are not dropping your elbow in the middle of the throw. |
| The ball leaves my hand at about the level of my shoulder. | Try throwing the ball farther. Feel the follow through of your hand. |
| When the ball leaves my hand I feel my wrist come into play. | Good observation. Use this in your backstroke. A little flip of the wrist at the very end of the stroke is just what you want. |

## RECOVERY DRILLS

The recovery in backstroke makes a perfect arch over the shoulder, starting from the point when the arm is straight along the side of the body and ending at the point when the arm is extended over-head. During this arch the muscles of the arm should be very loose and relaxed, and the elbow should be locked. Done well, the back-stroke recovery can provide four things: rest for the recovering arm, balance to the underwater arm, momentum for the next stroke, and last but not least, important alignment in a stroke where you cannot see where you are going! Use the following drills to improve your recovery technique for backstroke.

## 38. RELEASE TO RECOVER

### The purpose of this drill

- Making a clean transition to the recovery
- Avoiding drag when the hand leaves the water
- Learning to let go of the water

### How to do this drill

Step 1: Stand in chest deep water with your arms at your sides. Position your hands so the backs of your hands face the front. Without bending your elbows, quickly raise your hands out of the water. Notice that the water feels heavy against the backs of your hands. Notice that you carry a lot of water up as your hands leave the water.

Step 2: Now, with your arms at your sides, position your hands so the palms of your hands face the front. Without bending your elbows, quickly raise your hands out of the water. Notice that the water feels heavy against your palms. Notice that you carry a lot of water up as your hands leave the water. Try it again.

Step 3: Next, with your arms at your sides, position your hands so the palms of your hands face the outsides of your legs. Without bending your elbows, quickly raise your hands out of the water. Notice that your hands slide easily out of the water. Notice that you carry much less water up as your hands leave the water. Try it again.

Step 4: Finally, with your arms at your sides, position your hands so the backs of your hands face the outsides of your legs—pinkies forward. Without bending your elbows, quickly raise your hands out of the water. Notice that your hands slide easily out of the water. Notice that you carry much less water up as your hands leave the water. Try it again.

Step 5: Using what you learned from this exercise, swim backstroke focusing on making a clean exit from the water at the end of the underwater stroke, and a performing a swift but effortless recovery from the start. To accomplish this, you must select the hand position from Step 4 or 5 of this drill. Which one works best for you? Which one allows you to release the water best and produce a strong but relaxed recovery from start to finish?

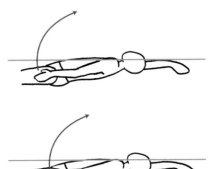

Figure 38: Two ways of releasing the water before recovery: thumb leading or pinkie leading

## Drill feedback chart

| PROBLEM | MODIFICATION |
|---|---|
| Releasing the water with my palm facing my leg works best for me, but then I am positioned to enter the water thumb first, instead of pinkie first. | Good observation. Backstrokers who use this release position are taught to flip their hand over in mid recovery so it is positioned for the ideal pinkie first entry. |
| Releasing the water with my palms out and pinkies up works best for me, but it only works if I roll the recovering side of my body up first. | Yes! Although less common, this release position makes use of the roll that is already happening in the stroke and allows a more direct recovery line as there is no need to flip the hand over in mid recovery. |
| My hand comes out of the water palm down, but it doesn't carry a lot of water up into the recovery because it is already at the surface. | Make sure you are getting all you can from the finish of the stroke and not cutting it short. The finish is the most productive part of the stroke in term of moving you forward. Ideally your hand will finish underwater, below the hip, so finding a way to slide it out of the water without lifting water up is important. |

# **39.** NON-STOP RECOVERY

## The purpose of this drill

- Utilizing recovery momentum
- Creating a counter balance to the underwater arm
- Maintaining stroke rhythm

## How to do this drill

Step 1: Swim backstroke for several laps. Focus on making a deep catch, then throwing the water up and past your shoulder in an accelerating pull/push motion. Feel your hand release the water then recover in a relaxed arch back to the start. Feel the rhythm and balance of the stroke. Notice that your arms work in opposition, that is when one is in mid recovery, the other is in mid stroke underwater—at the transition from pull to push.

Step 2: Now, after several rhythmic stroke cycles, stop your recovering arm at the top of the arch, when it is pointing up to the sky. Notice that when you do this it is difficult to keep accelerating the underwater arm. Try it again, several times. Notice that even though your recovering arm is not in the water moving your forward, that an interruption in the line and flow of the recovery affects your forward motion.

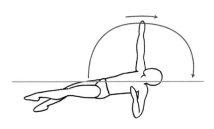

*Figure 39: Avoid slowing at the high point of the recovery arch*

Step 3: Swim backstroke again. Focus on the top of the arch of your recovery. Make sure have carried speed into your recovery. Make sure there is no slowing at the highest point. Feel the momentum of your recovering arm assist the stroking arm. Feel your recovery give rhythm to your stroke.

## Drill feedback chart

| PROBLEM | MODIFICATION |
| --- | --- |
| My arms are not opposite. | It is very important to establish opposition in the arm stroke. Focus on the home base position of one arm up and the other down, when one arm is entering the water at the same time that the other is exiting the water. Hit that point in every single stroke. Practice a lot to bring opposition into your stroke. |
| I don't seem to be able to bring speed into my recovery. | Make sure you are not stalling when your hand is at your side. It is important to establish and maintain a rhythmic stroke action in backstroke. |
| I can't relax my recovery and make it fast at the same time. | Try lifting your arm into recovery from the shoulder rather than from the hand. This will allow your hand and arm to rest while utilizing the core of your body to generate power and speed. |

# 40. ELEVEN O'CLOCK AND ONE O'CLOCK

## The purpose of this drill

- Feeling good alignment
- Avoiding under and over-reaching
- Alleviating shoulder stress

## How to do this drill

Step 1: Stand in front of a full-length mirror. Raise your left arm up as you would in the backstroke recovery until it is fully extended over your head. Notice how your hand aligns. If your arm were the hour hand on a clock, what time would it be? If your hand is pointing to twelve o'clock, you are over-reaching. If your hand is pointing to ten o'clock, you are under-reaching. If your hand is pointing to eleven o'clock, it is aligned with your shoulder, as it should be for backstroke.

Step 2: In order for the shoulder to rotate freely through the joint throughout the stroke, it must be aligned correctly in recovery. A poorly aligned backstroke recovery leads you to swim the whole stroke flat to avoid shoulder pain that occurs when the shoulder is forced to rotate in ways it was not intended to rotate, including performing a deep catch. Try it again. Raise your left arm up to eleven o'clock. Repeat several times. Try it with your right arm. Reach to one o'clock. Repeat several times.

Step 3: Now, standing in front of the mirror, arms at your sides, close your eyes. Raise your left arm, simulating the backstroke recovery. Try to finish the recovery at exactly eleven o'clock. Open your eyes and check your placement. Try again several times. Try it with your right

Figure 40: Enter at eleven o'clock with your left hand, and at one o'clock with your right hand

arm. With your eyes closed, try to finish your recovery at one o'clock exactly. Open your eyes and check your placement. Try again several times. Align your arm so you know where you are placing your hand.

Step 4: Keeping this exercise in mind, get in the pool and swim backstroke. Focus on achieving a well-aligned recovery. Know where you are placing your hand.

Recover with your left hand landing at eleven o'clock. Recover with your right hand landing at one o'clock. Feel your shoulder rotate freely into a deep catch position. Feel yourself travel straight down the lane.

## Drill feedback chart

| PROBLEM | MODIFICATION |
| --- | --- |
| My shoulders are very flexible, so I naturally over-reach. | It would still be better to aim for eleven o'clock and one o'clock to avoid a fish-tailing effect that occurs when you start your stroke aligned the center line of your body instead of your shoulders. |
| My left arm aligns correctly above my shoulder, but my right arm is way off. | Practice in the mirror more, first with your eyes open, then with your eyes closed. Be sure to open your eyes and check your placement. This immediate feedback will help you make adjustments. Practice until you know where your arm will land. |
| I am still swimming crooked! | Make sure you are catching at the same depth with each hand. |

## **41.** FIRM ELBOW, LOOSE WRIST

### The purpose of this drill

- Achieving an aligned recovery
- Achieving rest for the recovering arm
- Developing a productive recovery

### How to do this drill

Step 1: Get in the water and float on your back with your arms at your sides. Create forward movement by kicking productively.

Step 2: Raise your right arm, as you would in the backstroke recovery to the highest point in the recovery arch, so your hand is pointing to the sky. Let your body float with your right side higher than your left. Lock your elbow using your bones, not your muscles. Check that it is locked by gently shaking your arm from the shoulder for several seconds. Your arm should be straight from shoulder to wrist.

Step 3: Still kicking productively, with your right arm high, and your elbow locked, let your right hand go limp from the wrist. Check to see if your hand and wrist are relaxed by gently shaking your arm from the shoulder for several seconds. It should naturally flop to the outside, with your palm down. Switch arms and repeat.

Step 4: Now try swimming backstroke. Focus on maintaining a firm elbow and loose wrist throughout the recovery. Every seventh stroke, freeze your armstroke when your recovering arm at the high point of the recovery arch. Maintain forward motion with your kick.

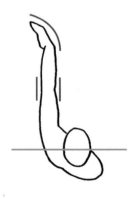

*Figure 41: Recover with your elbow locked and your hand limp from the wrist*

Check if your elbow is locked and your wrist and hand are relaxed by gently shaking your arm from the shoulder for several seconds. Your arm should be straight from shoulder to wrist, and your hand should flop outward, palm down. Resume swimming backstroke.

## Drill feedback chart

| PROBLEM | MODIFICATION |
| --- | --- |
| I sink when I stop my stroke with my arm in the air. | Use a faster kick to maintain forward momentum. Float with the non-recovering side of your body lower in the water. |
| I don't know how to lock my elbow. | It is as if you in school and were raising your hand in a way that you really wanted to the teacher to call on you. |
| My hand flops inward—palm up. | It takes muscles in your forearm to be engaged for your hand to be in this position. Practice using no muscles at all. |

## BREATHING DRILLS

When swimmers were asked about their favorite part of backstroke, the most common answer revolved around breathing not being issue because the face is out of the water. But, in fact, in backstroke breathing is an issue. It is an issue of rhythm and especially of energy management. Just as in all other strokes, and other sports, rhythmic breathing is essential in fueling the body to perform. Although it is tempting, the swimmer should never hold his or her breath in backstroke, but instead develop a breathing pattern of inhaling and exhaling. Good breathing technique makes a huge difference in backstroke. Use the following drills to improve your breathing technique for backstroke.

## 42. NOSE BREATHING/MOUTH BREATHING

### The purpose of this drill

- Understanding breathing issues in backstroke
- Learning to keep water out of the nose and mouth
- Experiencing rhythmic breathing in the water

### How to do this drill

Step 1: In chest deep water, take a big breath and lower yourself under the water until your nose is submerged, but your eyes are still out of the water. Expel air through your nose, but not your mouth in a long, continuous stream. Notice a steady stream of bubbles emerge from your nostrils. Stand and inhale through your mouth only. Submerge again, expelling air through your nose.

Step 2: Repeat ten times using your normal breathing rhythm. Submerge and exhale through your nose. Stand and inhale through your mouth. Notice that no water goes into your nose as long as bubbles are coming out. Repeat again, this time expelling air through your nose and mouth, and inhaling only through your mouth only. Be rhythmic.

Step 3: Now, get into a back float position. Take a big breath and allow yourself to slowly submerge. An instant before your nose goes underwater, begin actively expelling air through it. Notice the stream of bubbles coming from your nose. Notice that even in a head back position no water goes into your nose as long as bubbles are coming out.

Step 4: Now begin swimming backstroke. Focus on establishing a breathing rhythm. Inhale as one arm recovers, and exhale as the other recovers. Inhale through your mouth only. Exhale through your nose and mouth. Be sensitive to the rhythm of the water splashing on to your face. Be prepared to expel air through your nose if the water approaches. Keep the exchange of air going, and keep the water out.

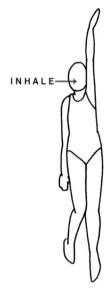

INHALE→

EXHALE

Figure 42a: Inhale through your mouth as one arm recovers

Figure 42b: Exhale through your nose and mouth as the other arm recovers

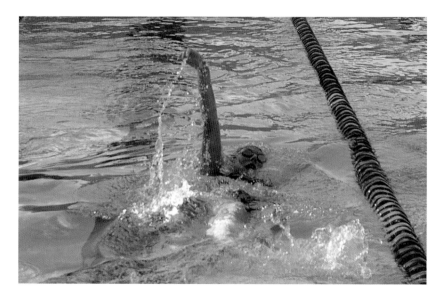

## Drill feedback chart

| PROBLEM | MODIFICATION |
|---|---|
| Why do I need to exhale through my nose and mouth? | Air can be expelled more quickly through the mouth than the nose. Since there is a limited window in which you can expel air, you want to make sure you are getting rid of all the old air to make room for new air. The main reason you expel air through your nose is to keep water out. |
| I still get water in my nose. | Make sure you start expelling air through your nose before your nose is submerged. Make sure you are not using your nose to inhale. |
| Isn't it easier to just wear a nose plug? | That is a solution to water getting in your nose. But rhythmic breathing should still be a part of your backstroke. |

# **43.** FUEL YOUR STROKE

## The purpose of this drill

- Understanding fueling the body in backstroke
- Learning to inhale deep
- Learning to exhale long

## How to do this drill

Step 1: In streamline position, kick backstroke across the pool rapidly. Use a fast kick rhythm. Kick strongly. Notice you are out of breath when you get to the other side of the pool. Backstroke is the only stroke where the power phase of the kick is against gravity. A great deal of oxygen is needed to sustain the kick. Kick another lap, actively and rhythmically inhaling new air and exhaling old air.

Step 2: Swim backstroke across the pool rapidly. Use a quick stroke rhythm. Notice you are out of breath when you get to the other side of the pool. The path of backstroke arm is the longest of all strokes. A great deal of oxygen is needed to sustain the stroke. Swim another lap, actively and rhythmically inhaling new air and exhaling old air.

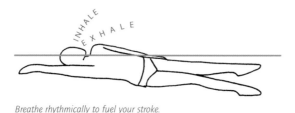

*Breathe rhythmically to fuel your stroke.*

Step 3: Swim backstroke again. Focus on the rhythm of your breathing. In order to best fuel the stroke, you must establish and maintain a breathing rhythm. You must learn to inhale quick and deep, and exhale long and continuously. Try it again. With the recovery of one arm, refuel by inhaling quick and deep. With the recovery of the other arm, exhale long and continuously to make room for new fuel.

## Drill feedback chart

| PROBLEM | MODIFICATION |
| --- | --- |
| So there is a good reason that I feel backstroke is the most tiring stroke? | Yes, it is oxygen-intensive. In fact, studies have shown that backstroke burns the most calories of any stroke. This is why it is so important to learn to breath productively for backstroke. |
| I tend to hold my breath in backstroke. | To keep your body fueled to perform the backstroke, you must avoid holding your breath, and actively keep expelling used air and replacing it with new fuel. |
| Why is the inhale quick and the exhale long? | The inhale is quick and deep to fill the lungs as quickly as possible with new air so the muscles can be fueled. The exhale is long for two reasons: first, expelling air assists the power motions of the stroke, and second, you want to make sure to get rid of all the old air, to make room for as much new fuel as possible. |

## LEVERAGE DRILLS

A good backstroke depends on leverage. Without it, more speed can only be achieved through a faster stroke rate and kick, and this is limiting factor. The main source of leverage in backstroke is the body roll. Powered by the swimmer's core, the body roll not only provides more potential power and speed to the arm stroke, but it also increases the swimmer's range of motion. By using leverage from the core in backstroke, fewer strokes are necessary, more distance per stroke can be realized, and less energy is expended. Use the following drills to improve your leverage in backstroke.

## 44. HIP TO HIP

### The purpose of this drill

- Learning to initiate the roll from the hip
- Feeling the center of power for the backstroke
- Developing rhythmic hip rotation

### How to do this drill

Step 1: Float on your back with your arms at your sides. Use a gentle but continuous kick to produce forward motion. Using your hips only, rotate your body to the right about 45 degrees and hold for the count of six. Using your hips only, rotate your body to the left about 45 degrees and hold for the count of six. Continue for several laps.

Step 2: Now float on your back with your left arm at your side and your right arm extended above your head. Using your hips only, rotate your body about 45 degrees towards the extended arm and hold for the count of six. Using your hips only, rotate your body to the right about 45 degrees as you move your extended arm through the path of the stroke to your side, and move the arm at your side along the back-stroke recovery path to the extended position. Hold for the count of six. Rotate again to the left as your switch arm positions. Continue for several laps. Feel your body balance shift.

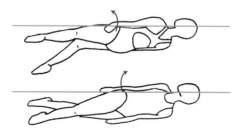

Step 3: Now swim regular back-stroke. As your left arm enters the water, use your hips to rotate your body about 45 degrees towards that arm. As your right arm enters the water, use your hips to rotate your body to the

Figure 44: Rotate from hip to hip

right about 45 degrees towards that arm. Continue for several laps. Feel your body balance shift. Feel the power as you rotate hip to hip.

Step 4: Swim backstroke again using your hips to rotate your body towards the arm entering the water. Feel your arm driven down to the catch position. Feel the rhythm produced through your hip to hip motion. Notice that as your hip rotates your body down to enter the water, your opposite hip is rotated up and is assisting your arm gain speed as it goes into the recovery. Keep swimming backstroke using your hips to your advantage on both sides of your body.

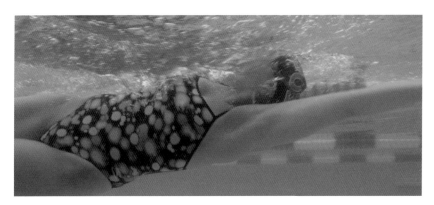

## Drill feedback chart

| PROBLEM | MODIFICATION |
| --- | --- |
| When my hips rotate, I feel unstable in the water. | It is difficult at first to get used to floating in a position other than flat. Give it more practice. Learn to depend on the muscles of your core to provide stability. |
| So, you should never be flat in backstroke, correct? | Only for the brief moment that your body is in the very middle of moving to balance on your other hip. |
| My feet rotate as well as my body. | That is okay. Flutter kick works in any position. |

## **45.** THE INDEPENDENT HEAD

### The purpose of this drill

- Establishing a stable head position
- Learning to isolate movement
- Feeling a relaxed neck

### How to do this drill

Step 1: Float on your back with your arms at your sides. Use a continuous kick to produce forward motion. Without moving your head, rotate your body to the right about 45 degrees and hold for the count of six. Notice that your left shoulder rises and becomes closer to the left side of your face. Without moving your head, rotate your body to the left about 45 degrees and hold for the count of six. Notice that your right shoulder rises and becomes closer to the right side of your face. Repeat. Continue for several laps.

Step 2: Next, floating on your back with your arms at your sides and kicking for forward motion, rotate your body to the right about 45 degrees and to the left about 45 degrees at one-second intervals. Make sure your head stays still by consciously relaxing your neck so your body does not carry your head along in its rotation. Feel the raised shoulder approach the side of your face. Feel the other shoulder move away from your face. Feel your head floating still in the middle of your rhythmic rotation. Repeat. Continue for several laps.

Step 3: Now, swim regular backstroke with good hip rotation and keeping your head very still and your neck deliberately

*Figure 45: Keep your head still by relaxing your neck so your body does not carry your head along in its rotation.*

relaxed. With every arm entry, rotate your body from the hips towards that arm. Feel your opposite shoulder rise nearing the side of your face. Feel your head float as if it was independent of your body in front of you.

**Drill feedback chart**

| PROBLEM | MODIFICATION |
|---|---|
| I can't relax my neck. | Try lowering your shoulders to relax the muscles in your neck. Practice on land and then again in the water. |
| I can't tell if my head is staying still in the water. | Focus on the water level around your ears. It should stay the same with your ears under the water at all times. |
| I feel I get more power when my head moves with my body. | Unfortunately the drag produced by your head moving cancels out any gain. |

## 46. THE PERFECT ANGLE

### The purpose of this drill

- Utilizing core leverage
- Producing leverage in the mid-pull
- Feeling a stable elbow

### How to do this drill

Step 1: Swim backstroke. As your body rotates in and out of the stroke focus on the leverage produced from your core. Notice how it positively affects every phase of your stroke. It sends your hand into the catch with force. It assists your arm stoking up and past your shoulder. It helps you finish fast. It drives your arm into the recovery with speed. As you are swimming, notice each of these points of leverage from the core working in your stroke.

Step 2: Continuing to swim backstroke, focus on the point in your stroke when your arm is in mid-pull underwater. This is the point when your elbow reaches a maximum bend, as it transitions from a pulling motion to a pushing motion. It is also the point when your body is rotated down towards your stroking side. Feel the rotation in your body. Feel the angle of your arm bent at the elbow.

Step 3: Continue swimming backstroke. Focus on keeping your elbow high and stable at the mid point in the stroke. At this point, when the elbow is at its maximum angle, and if it is aligned correctly with the shoulder and hand, a perfectly

*Figure 46: Correctly aligned at the midpoint of the stroke, a straight line appears from the elbow of the stroking arm through the chest to the opposite shoulder*

straight line appears from the elbow to the shoulder, through the chest and all the way to the opposite shoulder. Swim backstroke finding the perfect angle for leverage at the mid-pull in each stroke.

## Drill feedback chart

| PROBLEM | MODIFICATION |
| --- | --- |
| My body is flat at the mid-point of my stroke. | To benefit from leverage at this important phase of the stroke, your body should be rotated towards your stroking arm. |
| My hand, elbow and shoulder line up in the mid-pull, but my arm is pretty straight. | When the hand is far away from the body in the mid-pull it is not as strong. Try to increase the bend in your elbow without sacrificing your alignment. |
| I don't feel the line from my elbow to my opposite shoulder. | Focus on the end points of the line: the elbow and the opposite shoulder. Make sure you elbow is firm. Hold it firmly at a right angle to the body as your body leans towards it. |

## COORDINATION DRILLS

When all the elements of backstroke work together, they create a smooth, rhythmic stroke that carries the swimmer gracefully through the pool with seemingly little effort. Good backstroke coordination is more that simply doing things in the right sequence. It requires the swimmer to use the opposition inherent in the stroke to balance the actions of both sides of the body so they work interdependently throughout the stroke. Use the following drills to improve your coordination in backstroke.

## **47.** HOME BASE CHECKPOINT

### The purpose of this drill

- Checking coordination
- Maintaining opposition
- Swimming tall

### How to do this drill

Step 1: Swim backstroke at a relaxed rate. Focus on the opposition in your stroke. Start from the point when one arm is extended over your head, and the other is at your side—exactly opposite of the other arm, when you are at your tallest, do your arms remain opposite throughout the rest of the stroke cycle? Practice for several laps.

Step 2: Swim backstroke at a faster rate focusing on the opposition in your stroke. Use your tall position—that is the point when one arm is extended over your head, and the other is at your side—exactly opposite of the other arm as your home base position. Every sixth stroke, check to see if you are maintaining opposition in your stroke at this home base position.

Step 3: Sprint backstroke. Focus on the opposition in your stroke. Are you able to hit the home base position each stroke? Are you swimming tall? Practice Steps 1 - 3 several times.

*Figure 48: Maintain opposition with each stroke by hitting your homebase position*

Drill feedback chart

| PROBLEM | MODIFICATION |
| --- | --- |
| My home base position seems to be with both arms at my sides. | This means you are not benefiting from the opposition of the stroke because one arm is doing a complete stroke before the other arm starts. Try keeping both arms moving at all times. |
| I don't feel tall at the home base position. | Make sure your elbows are locked through the recovery and entry so you are at your tallest at the home base position. |
| When I sprint I lose the home base position. | Some loss of efficiency is expected when you sprint, but the longer you can maintain opposition and height while you are sprinting the better your speed potential will be. |

## **48.** FIND YOUR X

### The purpose of this drill

- Feeling cross-stroke balance
- Establishing stroke stability
- Kicking up at the catch

### How to do this drill

Step 1: Swim backstroke emphasizing rotation from the hips. Establish rhythm from the hips. Create leverage from the hips. Drive your arm stroke from the hips. And feel that your kick is assisted by your hip rotation. Your hips are central to all other stroke actions.

Step 2: Continue swimming backstroke. Notice that when your hips are rotated left to the maximum, your left arm is driving deep to the catch. At the same time, your right foot should be kicking up, creating a cross-stroke line. Feel your kick assist your catch.

Step 3: Continue swimming backstroke. Notice that when your hips are rotated right to the maximum, that your right arm is driving deep to the catch. At the same time, your left foot should be kicking up, creating a cross-stroke line. Feel your kick assist your catch.

Step 4: Swim backstroke hitting this cross-stroke balance point with each stroke. Make one stroke of an X when your left hip is rotated down, and the other stroke of the X when your right hip is rotated down. Your hips will be the center point.

*Figure 48: Hit the cross-stroke balance point with each stroke*

## Drill feedback chart

| PROBLEM | MODIFICATION |
| --- | --- |
| My opposite foot is kicking down when I catch. | That means that your same side foot is kicking up. This is not as common, but it still assists the catch of the stroke if timed perfectly. |
| I don't feel that my hip rotation assists by kick. | As your hip rises, allow it to draw your thigh and knee up with it, then snap the top of your foot upward to complete the kick. |
| I feel that my shoulders are the center point of my backstroke. | This means that your hips are probably floating flat, and not assisting your stroke as they could. Try initiating your rotation from the hips and let your shoulders follow. |

## **49.** BACKSTROKE SILHOUETTE

### The purpose of this drill

- Feeling your space in the water
- Maintaining full alignment
- Balancing efficiency and drag

### How to do this drill

Step 1: Swim backstroke focusing on the your spine line. Feel your feet align with your head. Feel the space that you take up in the water. This is your backstroke silhouette. Where is it widest? Where is it narrowest? Is it streamlined? Is there a purpose for the wide part? Is there a way to make the widest point in your stroke narrower to reduce drag without reducing your efficiency?

Step 2: Imagine you had no elbows, and you could only use a straight-arm stroke. Knowing that the completely circular backstroke path, both over and under the water is inefficient and hard on the shoulders, choose the path to the side of your body. Try it, perform the backstroke with straight arms, stroking to the sides of your body, as if you were making a snow angel. Notice that your feet sway toward your underwater arm with every straight-arm stroke. Feel the drag that is created by your feet fishtailing. Feel that the space you take up in the water is much larger. Try it again.

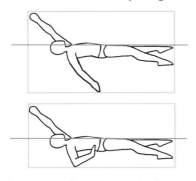

Step 3: Return to backstroke with elbows and regain your narrower arm stroke. Regain your head to toe alignment. Regain your smaller, more streamlined backstroke silhouette.

*Figure 49: Maintain a small backstroke silhouette*

## Drill feedback chart

| PROBLEM | MODIFICATION |
| --- | --- |
| With the straight-arm stroke, If I kick hard, my feet don't fishtail. | When you use your kick to overcome the drag that your fishtailing legs produce, it is not helping your move forward. |
| Even with a bending elbow, my silhouette is still wide during the mid-pull. | Yes, that is the widest part of your silhouette, however, there is a good reason for it. At that point you are producing more power than drag. |
| So, for the most streamlined backstroke I should make my arm stroke as narrow as possible? | You want your backstroke to be as narrow as it can be without reducing your stroke efficiency. If you make your mid-stroke narrower than a right angle, although your silhouette will be smaller, you will loose power in your stroke. It is a delicate balance. |

# 50. CORE STABILITY/CORE POWER

## The purpose of this drill

- Understanding the two roles of the core
- Feeling the effects of core stability
- Feeling the effects of core power

## How to do this drill

Step 1: Swim backstroke. Emphasize hip rotation. Focus on the point in your stroke when your left arm is catching deep underwater, and your right hand is starting the recovery. Feel the tension in your core affect both sides of your stroke. Simultaneously, the muscles of your core are driving the left side of your body down to make a solid catch, and, providing stability to the right arm as it travels into the air.

*Figure 50a: The core provides stability to the recovering arm*

*Figure 50b: The core provides power to the stroking arm*

Step 2: Continue swimming backstroke. Focus on the point in your stroke when your left arm is in mid-pull, and your right hand is moving at the top of the recovery arch. Feel the tension in your core affect both sides of your stroke. Simultaneously, the muscles of your core are powering the transition from pull to push as the left hand sweeps past the shoulder and elbow, and, providing balance to the right arm as it reaches the recovery's highest point.

Step 3: Continue swimming backstroke. Focus on the point in your stroke when your left arm is finishing the underwater stroke, and your right hand is preparing to enter the water. Feel the tension in your core affect both sides of your stroke. Simultaneously, the muscles of your core are adding speed to the left arm as it accelerates towards the end of the underwater stroke, and, providing alignment to the right arm as it sets up to cut through the surface of the water.

## Drill feedback chart

| PROBLEM | MODIFICATION |
| --- | --- |
| I don't feel the difference between core power and core stability. | Core stability is more subtle than core power, however it is just as important. Core power actively initiates movement, whereas as core stability provides tension that controls movement. |
| Which muscles in my core are most important to backstroke? | All of them, especially the rhomboids, lats, obliques and the rectus abdominus, which are some of the largest muscles of the core. |
| So, it seems that the same muscles can provide power and stability. | Yes, they can do both at different points in the stroke. |

## DRILLS FOR BREASTSTROKE

## BODY POSITION DRILLS

Unlike the freestyle and backstroke that use latitudinal rotation for leverage and power, the breaststroke depends on a longitudinal motion. This means that the floating position of breaststroke is not simply oriented forward, it alternates between a downward leaning position and an upward leaning position.

This stroke feature can enhance the productivity of the breaststroke dramatically if done correctly. It can also produce significant drag in a stroke that already has several potential points of drag, therefore achieving good body position in breaststroke is a major priority. Use the following drills to improve your body position in breaststroke.

## 51. TWO BALANCE POINTS

### The purpose of this drill

- Understanding breaststroke body position
- Feeling the downward balance point
- xFeeling the upward balance point

### How to do this drill

Step 1: Take a big breath and float face down in the water with your arms at your sides. Look at the bottom of the pool, not forward. Press your chest down in the water so you hips feel light and float higher than your chest. This is the downward balance point for breaststroke.

Step 2: Again, take a big breath and float face down with your arms at your sides. Look at the bottom of the pool, not forward. Holding your hips stable, raise your chest above your hips. This is the upward balance point for breaststroke.

Step 3: Again, take a big breath, float face down, arms at your sides and look at the bottom of the pool. Achieve the downward balance point and hold for the count of three. Then, achieve the upward balance point and hold for the count of three.

Notice that it is more difficult to hold the upward balance point for the count of three. Try it again. Press your chest down and find the downward balance point, then raise your chest to find the upward balance point.

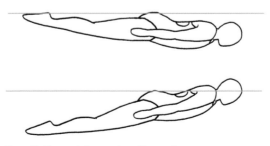

Figure 51: The two balance points of breaststroke

Step 4: Once again, big breath, float with your arms at your sides looking at the bottom of the pool. Achieve the downward balance point and hold for the count of three then achieve the upward balance point. Repeat several times in a row, switching from balance point to balance point. Spend twice as long in the downward floating position than the upward floating position.

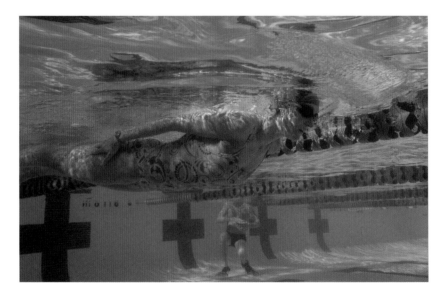

### Drill feedback chart

| PROBLEM | MODIFICATION |
| --- | --- |
| My legs sink when I am at the upward balance point. | Try raising your heels a bit when you hit the upward balance point. |
| My legs sink when I am at the downward balance point. | You might be jack-knifing at the hips. Instead, isolate the action to your upper body. Press your chest down gently, and allow your legs to float relaxed. |
| So, do I understand it correctly that the hips don't move? | Correct! The chest rises and descends while the hips remain stable. |

## **52.** LONG FLOAT

### The purpose of this drill

- Floating long and narrow
- Eliminating drag
- Feeling breaststroke's glide position

### How to do this drill

Step 1: Get in the pool and prepare to push off the wall for breaststroke. As you submerge under the water with your feet on the wall, extend your arms over your head and look down at the bottom of the pool. Stretch your arms until your elbows are straight. Squeeze your ears between your arms. Position your hands side by side so they form a point. Notice that this is similar to the streamline position for freestyle (Drill 3) except that the hands are positioned side by side for breaststroke, rather than clasped one over the over as in freestyle.

Step 2: Holding your arms tight in this position, push off the side of the pool into a front floating position. Look down at the bottom of the pool. Point your toes and stretch. Feel yourself cut through the water without resistance. Feel yourself float long and narrow. Repeat.

Step 3: Try it again. With your arms extended as long as possible over your head, squeezing your ears, place your hands side by side like a point.

*Figure 52: Float long and narrow during the glide phase*

Push off the wall and point your toes. Look at the bottom of the pool, not forward. Feel the momentum produced by your long float.

Step 4: Now, lower your chest and achieve your downward balance point for breast-stroke. Notice that your while your body aims downward, your streamlined arms aim straight ahead. Feel yourself float long. Feel yourself float narrow. Feel yourself perform the glide phase of the breaststroke. Repeat several times.

## Drill feedback chart

| PROBLEM | MODIFICATION |
| --- | --- |
| When I float downward with my body, my arms also point downward. | Try lifting your ribs a bit so you can achieve both the downward float for leverage and the streamline position for the forward alignment and glide of your stroke. |
| My hands don't really form a point when they are extended over my head. | Think of it as your streamlined leading edge. To be even more streamlined, try tucking your thumbs under your palms so you can line up your pointer fingers forward. |
| I can't see where I am going unless I looking forward. | Unfortunately you sacrifice your streamline position when you look forward because a lot of water bumps into your face, creating drag. Try practicing in un-crowded conditions and use the line on the bottom of the pool to direct you. If you must look forward, raise your eyes but do not raise your chin. |

## 53. SHORT FLOAT

### The purpose of this drill

- Achieving a quick short float
- Feeling breaststroke's breathing position
- Overcoming drag

### How to do this drill

Figure 53: Spend half as long in the short float position as in the long float position.

Step 1: Get in the pool and prepare to push off the wall for breaststroke. Submerge and extend your arms over your head, looking down at the bottom of the pool. As you push off the wall, achieve the breaststroke streamline position. Float long.

Step 2: Just before your momentum slows, simultaneously, raise your chest and draw your hands from the extended position toward your body and cross them over your chest. Notice that this action produces a bit of lift for your upper body, raising it toward the upward balance point. Try it again with more speed. Shift from the downward to the upward balance point by raising your upper body as you do a quick sweep of your hands to your chest.

Step 3: Notice that without changing your head position, your face rises through the surface of the water. This is your short float position, and the breathing position for breaststroke. Notice that you cannot easily sustain this position. Feel your face sink back into the water. Feel your feet sink. Try it again.

Step 4: Start from the beginning. Push off the wall in the breaststroke glide position, then achieve the downward balance point. Glide while you float long. Make your shift to the upward balance point quickly. Breathe during the short float. Return to the glide position before you start to sink. Repeat several times. Spend twice as long in the glide position as in the breathing position.

**Drill feedback chart**

| PROBLEM | MODIFICATION |
|---|---|
| I don't get enough lift to breathe when my hands move towards my chest. | Press down on the water slightly with your extended hands. Then raise your upper body as you sweep your hands quickly to your chest. |
| My forward motion stops when I shift to the breathing position. | Good observation. The short float or breathing position is the breaststroke position that creates the most drag. That is why you should spend half as much time in that position as in the long float or glide position. |
| My hips sink when I hit the breathing position. | It is very important not to raise your chin independently when you raise your upper body. Doing so changes the balance of the stroke, leading your hips to sink. |

## KICK DRILLS

The breaststroke kick stands alone among the other strokes in many ways. It is the only kick that generates its main power from the soles of the feet. It is the only kick that follows a circular kicking pattern. And, it is the only kick where the kick produces more power for forward motion than the arm stroke. The unique aspects of the breaststroke kick make it an especially interesting stroke for the technique-minded swimmer, and fun for the rest of us. Use the following drills to improve your kicking technique for breaststroke.

## 54. FOOT AWARENESS

### The purpose of this drill

- Learning breaststroke foot positions
- Practicing ankle rotation
- Feeling foot speed

### How to do this drill

Step 1: Sit in a straight-back chair. Raise your feet off the ground until there is no bend in your knees and your legs are extended in front of you. Focus on your feet and ankles. Your feet serve as your pushing surfaces in the breaststroke kick, and your ankles work to position your feet so they can perform the kick. Rotate your feet in a circle and feel the range of motion that is possible from your feet.

Step 2: Next, practice the basic foot position for the power phase of the breaststroke kick. Flex your feet by raising your toes toward you and turning your feet out to the sides. The entire soles of your feet should be available to push water around and back in a whip-like motion.

Step 3: Now, practice the foot position for the early part of the power phase of the breaststroke kick. From the flexed position, rotate your feet so that the inner surface, along the arch of your foot is available to push water out and around. This will be your leading edge during this part of the kick.

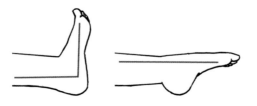

Step 4: Now, practice the foot position for the late part of the power phase of the breaststroke kick.

*Figure 54: Use your ankles to position your feet through the range of motion of the breaststroke kick*

From the flexed position, rotate your feet so that the outer edge of your foot is available to push water in and around. This will be your leading edge during this part of the kick.

Step 5: Next, practice the foot position for the glide phase of the breaststroke kick. Point your toes attempting to make a straight line from your knee to your toes. Allow your feet to turn inward if it is comfortable in order to make the most streamline shape possible.

Step 6: Now, try the complete foot rotation cycle. Flex your feet to prepare for the power phase. First position your flexed feet to push out and back by leading with the inner surface of your feet. Then position your flexed feet to push in and back by leading with the outer surface of your feet. Finally, point your toes as you would to complete the cycle in the glide position.

## Drill feedback chart

| PROBLEM | MODIFICATION |
| --- | --- |
| Flexing my feet does not come naturally. What is the trick? | It is as if you are walking on your heels with the balls of your feet off the ground and your toes curled upward. Try it. Feel the contraction along your shins. Feel the stretch in your calves. Practice this, as it is an essential foot position for breaststroke. |
| When I finish the power phase, the soles of my feet almost touch. | That shows excellent flexibility. Use this to your advantage for the end of the breaststroke kick. |
| I can't make a straight line from my knees to my toes. | As humans, we spend very little time with our feet pointed. Our everyday movements like walking and standing can leave our tendons unaccustomed to the point position. With practice however, toe point can be improved. |

## 55. AROUND THE KNEES

### The purpose of this drill

- Feeling the path of the breaststroke kick
- Maintaining a hold on the water
- Achieving foot speed

### How to do this drill

Step 1: Sit in a straight-back chair. Hold on to the sides of the chair for support. Raise your feet off the ground until there is no bend in your knees and your legs are extended in front of you. Prepare to trace the path of the breaststroke kick. Focus on your legs and your feet as they move through the phases of the kick in a mirror image of each other.

Step 2: From the extended leg position, begin with your toes pointed, as your would hold them in the streamline position. Now, draw your feet back as far as possible on either side of the chair. As your feet move back, curl your toes up and turn your feet outward to prepare for the power phase of the kick. Your legs should now be bent at the knee as far as possible, more than 90 degrees.

Step 3: Now, leading with the outside blades of your feet, press your feet outward and away from your body, holding your knees in a stable position. Then, when your feet are just wider than your shoulders, still holding your knees stable, rotate your feet so the inside blades lead and whip them inward and away from your body quickly until your legs are straight. At the very end of this rounded movement, point your toes again.

Step 4: Try it again. Draw your feet to the outsides of the chair as you flex them and turn them outwards, producing the maximum knee bend possible. Then, holding your knees still, push the soles of your feet outward and away from you leading with the outside blades of your feet. When your feet are wider than your shoulders, whip your feet quickly inward and back, leading with the inside blades of your feet until your legs are straight. Finish by pointing your toes. Notice that your feet have traveled a circular path around your knees.

Step 5: Now try it in the water. With your back against the side of the pool, hold on to the wall with your arms extended out from your sides for stability. Extend your legs in front of you and point your toes. With your knees remaining still, draw you feet back outside your knees to either side of you as you flex

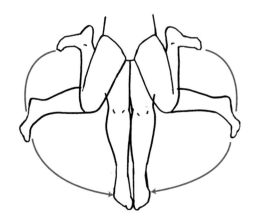

*Figure 55: Your feet should pivot around your knees*

your feet. Leading with the outside blades of your feet, press the water out and away from your body using the soles of your feet, then when they are at about shoulder width, whip them inward and away from you, leading with the inside blade of your feet, traveling a circle around your knees until your legs are straight. Point your toes. Feel the soles of your feet push against the water through the entire circular power phase. Feel your feet pivot around your knees. Feel your feet accelerate through the kick. Practice several times.

## Drill feedback chart

| PROBLEM | MODIFICATION |
|---|---|
| My knees don't stay still. | For the best kick, your knees should be still. Set your knees apart, but no wider than your shoulders. Now try the kick again. Circle your feet around your still knees. |
| It is difficult to turn my feet out to the side. | Practice doing it while standing. Focus on rotating from the ankles. Then practice in the horizontal position again. |
| I don't feel the lead with the blades of my feet. | The part of your feet leading the way around the circular path of the power phase changes from beginning to end. As your feet travel outward it is the outer edges of your foot. As your feet travel back inwards, it is the inside edges of your feet. Use ankle rotation to change the position your feet so they engage the water through the changing path of the kick. |

# 56. RECOVER FIRST

## The purpose of this drill

- Distinguishing the kick's power phase and recovery
- Recovering without drag
- Learning to release the water

## How to do this drill

Step 1: Using a kick board, float on your front and kick breaststroke kick across the pool. Hold the board so it supports your arms and allows you to float comfortably head up. As you kick, focus on your progress through the water. Is it consistent?

Step 2: First, draw your heels behind you and to the outside of your thighs as you position your feet into the flexed and turned out position. Do you move forward during this phase of the kick?

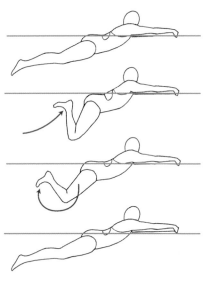

Step 3: Next, press the water back quickly around a circular path in a whip-like motion until your legs are straight. Do you move forward during this phase of the kick?

Step 4: Try it again. Draw your heel back and out behind you. This is the recovery of the breaststroke kick, when your feet are not creating forward motion, but moving into position for the power phase. Unlike in other swimming actions, in breaststroke kick the recovery comes before the power phase. During

*Figure 56: Achieve a gentle recovery and then an active power phase*

the recovery, your feet should not push water. They should gently slide through the water so they create as little drag as possible.

Step 5: The recovery ends when your feet reach their highest point behind you and are turned to the outside as much as possible. The power phase begins when you push the water back and around with the soles of your feet. During the power phase your feet should engage the water and hold on to it as they whip around until your legs are straight, moving you forward the whole time.

Step 6: Continue kicking breaststroke kick focusing on achieving a gentle recovery that does not create drag, then an active power phase that vaults you forward in the water.

## Drill feedback chart

| PROBLEM | MODIFICATION |
| --- | --- |
| I actually go backwards during the recovery. | This means your feet are engaging the water during the recovery and pulling you back. The recovery is a slow, gentle motion in which you try not push water, but instead slide your feet through the water, creating as little drag as possible. |
| I don't really move forward during the power phase. | Work on the flexed foot position. Your pushing surface is the sole of your foot. You must position it so it will be what pushes the water back and around. If your feet are not flexed by the start the power phase, you will not move forward. |
| I am floating uphill with the kickboard. | Modification: Press slightly down with your arms on the front of the kick board—that is the edge that is farthest away from you to correct your balance. |

## 57. STRAIGHT HIP LINE

### The purpose of this drill

- Using a stable hip position
- Avoiding bending at the hips
- Eliminating Drag

### How to do this drill

Step 1: Stand on the pool deck. Balance on your left foot. Raise you right foot off the ground without bending at the hip. How will you accomplish this? If you lift your knee in order to get your foot off the ground you will be bent at the hips. If you lift your foot straight up you will also be bent at the hips. Try lifting the heel of your foot behind you. Notice you have raised your foot without bending at the hips. Notice the straight line from your shoulder to your knee. Try it again.

Step 2: Achieving a breaststroke kick without bending at the hips is very important in avoiding a major potential point of drag in the stroke. Try it in the water. Float vertically in water deeper than you are tall. Place your hands across your chest and begin kicking breaststroke kick.

Step 3: Notice that if you begin the kick by raising your knees toward your chest, you sink immediately. Instead, raise your heels behind you toward your buttocks, creating a straight line from your shoulders to your knees. Notice that you don't sink.

Step 4: Continue kicking breaststroke kick in the vertical position. Keep your face from submerging by maintaining a straight line from shoulder to knee when you draw your heels back behind you.

Step 5: Now try kicking breaststroke kick in the horizontal position. Float on your front with your arms extended. To begin the kick, raise your heels behind you, keeping a straight line from shoulder to hip. Then whip your feet back and around. Notice that without bending at the hips you reduce drag and move forward better.

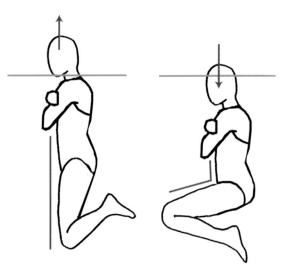

Figure 57: To reduce drag maintain a straight line from your shoulders to your knees

## Drill feedback chart

| PROBLEM | MODIFICATION |
|---|---|
| I bob up and down in the vertical position. | This probably means that you are creating drag by drawing your knees up, but are able to overcome it with a strong power phase. Just think how powerful your kick would be if you eliminated the drag point of your raised knees. |
| When I raise my heels behind me my knees come apart. Doesn't this create drag too? | As long as your knees stay within the profile of your shoulders it is fine. But if you start the kick motion with your knees slightly apart, they will probably remain more stable. |
| So your hips stay pretty still throughout the kick? | Yes, the hips should remain stable as your foot rotates around your knee. |

## **58.** FEET OUTSIDE KNEES

### The purpose of this drill

* Feeling stable knees
* Keeping the knees inside the feet
* Kicking around the knees

### How to do this drill

Step 1: Using a kickboard, float on your front and kick breaststroke kick across the pool. Hold the board so it supports your arms and allows you to float comfortably with your head up. Before you move your legs from the extended position, notice how your knees are aligned. They should be lined up with your hips, and they should stay in this position through the entire kick.

Step 2: Begin the kick by performing the recovery. Draw your feet back and to the outside of your legs then flex your feet preparing for the power phase. As you draw your feet back, check your knee position. Are your knees wider than your feet? If they are, stop and start over.

Step 3: Your feet must rise and move away from each other while your knees get wider, rather than moving your feet up the middle while your knees get wider and wider apart. Try it again. Raise your feet behind you and let them fall to the outside, flexing them at the very end of

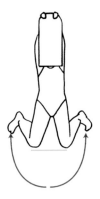

Figure 58a: Your feet should rise and move away from each other while your knees remain closer together

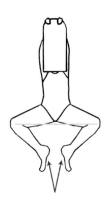

Figure 58b: Avoid moving your feet up the center as your knees get wider and wider

the recovery. Then engage the water with the soles of your feet and press the water out, around and back around your knees until your legs are straight. If you start the breaststroke kick with a good knee position, you will finish the kick with a powerful motion stabilized by your knees.

## Drill feedback chart

| PROBLEM | MODIFICATION |
| --- | --- |
| It seems awkward with my knees closer than my feet. | At first it will be awkward. After all, when in life do we do a movement similar to the breaststroke kick? With practice it will become easier. |
| My knees are aligned with shoulders. | That is fine if they remain stable throughout the kick. |
| It seems if I bring my feet up the middle in recovery, I create less drag. | You may create less drag with your feet, but you create much more drag with your wide knees and moving legs. |

## ARM STROKE DRILLS

Breaststroke arm stroke is unlike the arm stroke of any other stroke in terms of both path and purpose. Breaststroke arm stroke is relatively short compared to the other strokes, and it follows largely a lateral path. In terms of efficiency, breaststroke arm stroke produces the least forward motion of any stroke, and in fact it is the only stroke in which the kick produces more power than the arms. What the breaststroke arm stroke does do very well though is provide lift for the breathing, leverage for the kick, and rhythm for the stroke. Use the following drills to improve your arm stroke technique for breaststroke.

## 59. SWEEP OUT, SWEEP IN

### The purpose of this drill

- Learning the path of the breaststroke arms
- Using hand pitch
- Achieving lift

### How to do this drill

Step 1: Stand in waist-deep water. Bend forward at the hips so your chest and shoulders are in the water and your chin is on the surface of the water so you can observe your arms and hands throughout this drill. Extend your arms in front of you. Stretch from the elbows and position your hands in a point.

Step 2: Prepare to trace the path of the breaststroke arm stroke. With both arms moving in a mirror image of each other, pitch your hands slightly outward, thumbs down. Then, sweep your hands straight out just wider than your shoulders, remaining a few inches under the surface of the water.

Step 3: Now, flip your hands over so they are in a thumbs-up position, and sweep your hands inward and back towards your chest in a swift motion along a slightly deeper path in the water. Your hands should meet in the middle, palms together with your fingers pointing forward. Return your arms to the extended position and try it again.

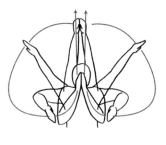

Figure 59: The path of the breastroke arm stroke

Step 4: From the starting point with your arms extended, sweep your hands out, thumbs down. From the widest point slightly outside your shoulders, reverse directions and sweep your hands in and back towards your upper chest, thumbs up. As you near the end of the insweep, allow your elbows to fold against your the sides of your rib cage. Return your hands to the extended position and do it again with more speed. Feel your hands press against the water. Feel the lift produced by the out and in sweep of the breaststroke arms.

## Drill feedback chart

| PROBLEM | MODIFICATION |
| --- | --- |
| I don't feel pressure against the water with my hands. | Try changing the pitch of your hands slightly. Also make sure your hands are traveling swiftly through the water, and accelerating throughout the stroke. |
| So, the breaststroke arm stroke is sort of like sculling. | Yes. It is a very lateral movement, and the hands flip over to reverse directions. The difference is that during the in sweep the hands do also move towards the chest at the same time as they are traveling inward. |
| This is all there is to the breaststroke arms... where does the forward motion come from? | The breaststroke arms produce very little forward motion. Instead their major contribution is adding lift to the stroke. |

# 60. HAIRPIN

## The purpose of this drill

- Holding on to the water as your hands change directions
- Changing the pitch of your hand
- Feeling lift

## How to do this drill

Step 1: Float face down in the water with your arms extended, hands forming a point. Do a gentle flutter kick to produce forward motion. Trace the path of the breaststroke arm stroke. Start by pitching your hands slightly palms-out and sweep the water to a point just wider than your shoulders. Then change the pitch of your hands to a palms-in position and sweep the water in and back towards your chest.

Step 2: Return to the extended position and try it again. Feel the water in your hands as you sweep out to the widest point. Hold on to the same water as your hands change directions in a tight turn, accelerating as you sweep in and towards your chest.

Figure 60: Hold on to the same water as you sweep in quickly from the widest point

Step 3: Try it again emphasizing the acceleration of your movement throughout the path of the arm stroke. Rotate your hands to pitch slightly out and sweep the water out to a point wider than your shoulders. As your hands make a hair pin turn, hold on to the water and gather speed as you sweep your hands quickly together and back towards your chest.

Step 4: Return your hands to the extended position and do it again. Press the water out and make a tight, hairpin turn and press the water in and back. Feel the lift achieved by your accelerating arm stroke. Do it again with enough speed to lift your face from the water on the insweep and catch a breath. Practice for several laps.

## Drill feedback chart

| PROBLEM | MODIFICATION |
| --- | --- |
| My hands make a wide turn, not a hairpin turn. | It is a very small space that you are dealing with. In order to gather speed enough speed to create lift, try to make a hairpin turn at the widest point. |
| I don't produce lift enough to breathe. | Practice holding on to the water and using more acceleration, especially as you sweep the water inward. |
| My hands sweep out, but then they go deep. | This means you are pressing the water down for lift. In order to avoid drag, it is very important that your hands use a lateral path, allowing your hands to go only about as deep as your chest. |

# 61. ACCELERATE AND ABBREVIATE

## The purpose of this drill

- Feeling lift
- Using hand speed
- Achieving a compact arm stroke

## How to do this drill

Step 1: Float face down in the water with your arms extended, hands forming a point. Do a gentle flutter kick to produce forward motion. Trace the path of the breaststroke arm stroke. Pitch your hands to sweep the water out just wider than your shoulders, then make a tight turn and sweep the water in and back towards your chest producing lift enough to get a quick breath.

Step 2: In order to avoid creating drag, your goal should be to create the smallest, quickest arm stroke possible that will produce enough lift so you can breathe. Try it again. With your arms extended, sweep out, make a hairpin turn and sweep in and back toward your chest quickly, so that your hands end up pointing forward under your chin as you catch a breath.

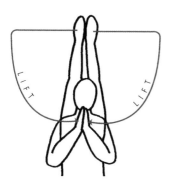

Step 3: Practice more, making your arm stroke as compact and quick as possible. Use the outsweep to gather speed and to position your hands to sweep in with a short burst of force that will lift your face out of the water to breathe. When sweeping inward with enough speed, you should be able to feel your forearms also pressing against the water. Practice for several laps.

*Figure 61: Create the smallest, quickest arm stroke possible that will produce enough lift to breathe*

## Drill feedback chart

| PROBLEM | MODIFICATION |
|---|---|
| When I sweep my hands out quickly, my fingertips break the surface of the water. | Pitch your hands downward a bit so they stay below the surface of the water while you are pressing the water outward. This is important in order to hold on to the water well. |
| In order to be compact should my stroke not go out as wide as my shoulders? | Your hands should still press out just wider than your shoulders. The areas you should try to make more compact are the turn at the widest point, and the depth and length of the insweep. |
| I don't feel my forearms pressing against the water. | You must produce enough speed squeezing the water together to feel this. Practice more. |

## 62. ELBOW GREASE

### The purpose of this drill

- Using a high elbow position
- Knowing when to fold the elbows in
- Avoiding drag

### How to do this drill

Step 1: Stand in waist-deep water. Bend forward at the hips so your chest and shoulders are in the water and your chin is on the water's surface so you can observe your arm movement throughout this drill. Extend your arms in front of you. Stretch from the elbows and position your hands in a point.

Step 2: Trace the path of the breaststroke arms. Sweep out beyond your shoulders maintaining straight elbows, then sweep in and back towards your chest maintaining a high elbow position. To achieve the high elbow position, your hands must move first, and your elbows must stay still until your hands are at the same width as your elbows. Try it several times focusing on your elbows.

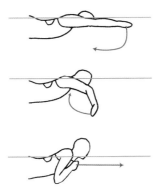

Step 3: Only as you hands come together at the end of the insweep should you allow your elbows to drop inward, in order to achieve a narrower shape in the water. Some swimmers bring their elbows in to the sides of their ribs, others bring their elbows and forearms together in front of their chest. Try both techniques. Which one works best for you?

Figure 63: Keep your elbows straight during the outsweep, high during the insweep and only allow them fold inward at the very end of the stroke

## Drill feedback chart

| PROBLEM | MODIFICATION |
| --- | --- |
| My elbows drop down on the insweep. | The high elbow position is important in all swimming strokes. In breaststroke, to get enough lift to breathe, you must keep your elbows high in the insweep. Practice it more. |
| My elbows stay high and wide even at the end of the arm stroke. | It is great that you can maintain high elbows, but to eliminate the drag that your elbows can cause at the end of the insweep, fold your elbows inward s a final step, giving yourself a narrower, more streamlined shape. |
| It seems that I make a narrower shape in the water if I bring my elbow and forearms together in front of my chest. | Good. Both these techniques work successfully for different swimmers. The benefit of your chosen technique is that your arms are already half way recovered at the end of your power phase. The benefit of the other technique is that the power phase is longer. |

## RECOVERY DRILLS

Like the other strokes, recovery in breaststroke brings the arms back to the starting position, traveling in the reverse direction of the power phase. But in breaststroke the recovery is unique because it happens underwater, making it a major source of drag in the stroke. Swimmers must practice being as streamlined as possible at this point in the stroke, and to perform the recovery quickly so that the effects of drag do not eliminate progress in their stroke. Use the following drills to improve your recovery technique in breaststroke.

## **63.** SPEED RECOVERY

### The purpose of this drill

- Practicing a quick recovery
- Transitioning from power phase to recovery
- Avoiding drag

### How to do this drill

Step 1: Float face down in the water with your arms extended, hands forming a point. Do a gentle flutter kick to produce forward motion. Trace the path of the breaststroke arm stroke. Sweep the water out and in and back towards your chest producing lift enough to get a quick breath. At the very end of the power phase, your palm should come together and your elbows should fold inward.

Step 2: At the point when you have achieved lift, near the end of the power phase, there is a temptation to stop moving your arms, but don't do it! Instead, continue to accelerate your arms into the recovery. In fact, the recovery should be the fastest part of your stroke. As your palms come together at the end of the insweep, extend your arms forward in a tight arrow to cut through the water with as little drag as possible, and producing the fastest movement of the arm stroke.

Step 3: Try it again. Make the arm stroke and recovery a three step, non-stop motion. Sweep the water out, then in, then accelerate through the recovery until your arms are extended straight in front of you at the starting point. Only when the arms return to the extended position do they stop. Try it several times.

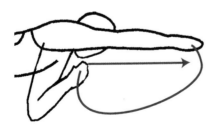

*Figure 63: Accelerate your arms into the recovery*

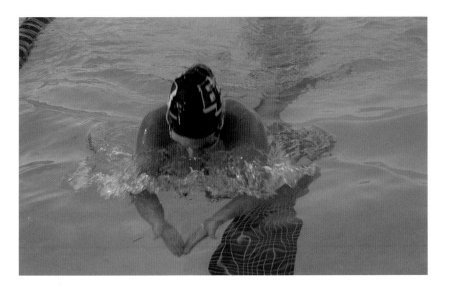

## Drill feedback chart

| PROBLEM | MODIFICATION |
|---------|--------------|
| My arms seem to get stuck at the end of the power phase. | Try pushing your elbow to straight as soon as your palms come together. |
| My arms break the surface of the water during the recovery. | That means you have achieved a great amount of lift. Some swimmers do recover over the water successfully, but take a great deal of energy to maintain for any distance. You should choose to recover either under the water or over the water, and not through the surface of the water that creates the most drag of all. |
| My palms do not come all the way together at the end of the power phase. | You might be missing out on some of your lift opportunity at the end of your insweep. Sweep your hands all the way together, both to get the most out of your power phase, and to be as fast and narrow as possible going into recovery in order to avoid drag. |

## **64.** GET BACK TO STREAMLINE

### The purpose of this drill

- Returning to the downward balance point
- Being streamlined for more time
- Eliminating drag

### How to do this drill

Step 1: Swim breaststroke. Start by sweeping your hands out, then quickly inward and back toward your chest achieving lift to breathe. As you breathe, slide your heels up behind you and to the outside, flexing your feet at the end. Accelerate your arms into the recovery returning your face to the water just before your hands reach the extended position. Kick out and around with the soles of your feet, returning your feet to the extended position just after your arms.

Step 2: Try it again. Sweep out and inward with your hands, and catch a breath. Slide your feet up and out and flex your feet. Move your arms through the recovery as your face goes back in the water. Kick out and around with the soles of your feet until your legs are straight. Notice that when your arms and legs get back to the streamline starting point, you continue moving through the water with no effort. This is the glide position of the breaststroke, and the downward balance point. It is the position with the least drag, and the position you want to spend the most time in.

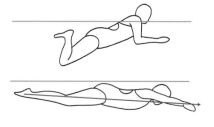

Step 3: Continue practicing breaststroke getting back to streamline with every stroke. Spend more time in the glide position than in all other phases

*Figure 64: Spend more time in the glide position than all the others put together*

of the stroke put together. Feel the momentum of the precious stroke move you forward during the glide.

## Drill feedback chart

| PROBLEM | MODIFICATION |
| --- | --- |
| So many things happen at the same time in breaststroke. | Just remember that the arms reach streamline before the legs, then glide. |
| I end up doing my arm stroke and kick at the same time. | Doing so can create too much drag to overcome. It works better to start the stroke with your arms and finish with your legs. |
| I don't produce much forward motion in my glide. | This could be caused by many issues but the most important problems to eliminate are kick inefficiency, and non-streamlined body position. |

## BREATHING DRILLS

The forward breathing position in the breaststroke can be a major source of drag when done incorrectly. If the line of the stroke is interrupted by an independent movement of the head, forward momentum is broken. Done correctly, breaststroke breathing requires no independent lifting of the head. This is achieved when the breathing happens within the arm stroke, and as a function of the body being at the upward balance point when it is time to inhale. As the upper body rises, the face naturally clears the water to breathe. Use the following drills to improve your breathing technique in breaststroke.

## 65. INHALE WITH THE INSWEEP

### The purpose of this drill

- Timing the inhale correctly
- Feeling lift
- Avoiding drag

### How to do this drill

Step 1: Swim breaststroke focusing on your two balance points. Start in the glide position leaning into the downward balance point. Feel your body move forward in the water with your hips higher than your chest. Now, begin the arm stroke by sweeping out, then in and back towards your chest. Feel the balance of your body change as you do the insweep. Feel your face rise as you produce lift with the insweep. Inhale when your body achieves the upward balance point.

Step 2: Draw your heels up and out and flex your feet as your arms go through the recovery. As you move into the power phase of the kick, your balance shifts again. Feel your face return to the water as you approach the downward balance point. Achieve streamline with your arms then your legs and glide.

*Figure 65: Inhale at the high point of the stroke, during the insweep*

Step 3: Try it again. Starting in the glide position, look down at the bottom of the pool. Begin your arm stroke and feel balance change and your face rise through the insweep. As you achieve the upward balance point, inhale. Notice that you did not have to lift your chin to breathe. It happened for you as a function of your stroke.

Step 4: Slide your feet into position for the power phase as you inhale and move your arms directly into the recovery. Kick and feel the balance of your body change

again towards the downward balance point, allowing your face to return to the water, and your arms achieve streamline followed shortly by your legs. Glide. Notice that you are again looking at the bottom of the pool without lowering your chin. Practice for several laps.

## Drill feedback chart

| PROBLEM | MODIFICATION |
|---|---|
| I don't stay at the upward balance point long enough to inhale. | There is a very small window of opportunity to inhale. Be sure you have exhaled all of your old air before your face rises, so that all you have to do is inhale at the high point. |
| My face doesn't clear the water enough to inhale if I don't lift my chin. | Rather than lifting your chin to achieve your inhale, which can interrupt your forward motion, try increasing the speed of your arm stroke to produce more lift, and make sure you are inhaling at the upward balance point, not before. |
| I am inhaling during the outsweep. | Although the outsweep produces some lift, it is the insweep that produces enough lift to pop your face out of the water without any other effort on your part. |

## 66. EXHALE WITH THE KICK

### The purpose of this drill

- Timing the exhale correctly
- Exhaling during the kick's power phase
- Emptying the lungs before the inhale

### How to do this drill

Step 1: Swim breaststroke focusing on your breathing rhythm. Inhale at the high point of the stroke, then exhale through the kick and glide. As with any physical effort, it is important to expel air during the period of highest effort. In the case of breaststroke, that is the power phase of the kick.

Step 2: Try it again. Inhale at the high point during the insweep. When your face returns to the water within the recovery, exhale as you kick out and around with force. Continue exhaling through the glide so that you expel all of your old air by the time your face rises for the next inhale.

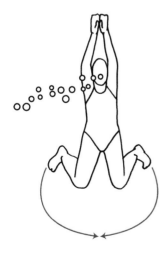

Step 3: Continue swimming breaststroke for several laps focusing on rhythmically exhaling with the power phase of the kick.

*Figure 66: Exhale during the power phase of the kick and during the glide*

195

## Drill feedback chart

| PROBLEM | MODIFICATION |
| --- | --- |
| I don't have enough air to exhale through the glide. | Practice controlling your exhale so that you finish expelling old air right before it is time to inhale. |
| What about exhaling during the arm stroke insweep... isn't that a major effort? | Since it is the kick that produces the most forward motion of the breaststroke, the exhale should be timed to happen then, but the final bit of exhale does actually happen at the insweep, to get rid of air remaining old air, right before the inhale. |
| I am exhaling during the arm stroke recovery. | The recovery overlaps with the power phase of the kick. |

# 67. NO NODDING!

## The purpose of this drill

- Maintaining a stable head position
- Achieving low profile breathing
- Avoiding lifting the chin to breathe

## How to do this drill

Step 1: Swim breaststroke focusing on maintaining a stable head position. Avoid any nodding action to achieve a breath. From the glide position, you should be looking at the bottom of the pool, not forward. Notice the position of your chin. It is neutral, not lowered or raised. It should remain neutral throughout the stroke.

Step 2: Begin the arm stroke by sweeping out. Feel your upper body begin to rise as your arm stroke produces lift. Feel your face begin to emerge from the water. Maintain your neutral chin as you do your quick insweep and feel your face pop out of the water without changing your chin position.

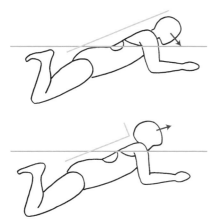

Step 3: You should be looking at the water while you inhale. As your arms move into recovery and your body shifts downward, your face will submerge and you should again be looking at the bottom of the pool.

Step 4: Continue swimming breaststroke, avoiding the nodding action to

*Figure 65: Hold the forward line of your stroke by looking down at the water while breathing*

breathe. Maintain a neutral chin position throughout the stroke. Never see the other side of the pool.

### Drill feedback chart

| PROBLEM | MODIFICATION |
|---|---|
| It seems that nodding helps me achieve my balance points. | When your head nods, your balance points become the top of your head and your chin, rather than the longer, stronger line from your head to your hips. |
| How do I know where I am if I can't look at the other side of the pool? | Use the line on the bottom of the pool to direct you. As you approach the wall, the line becomes a "T". |
| A lot of water flows down around my face when I look at the water while I am inhaling. | That is fine. You still have a large pocket of clear air in the middle to inhale. |

## LEVERAGE DRILLS

Breaststroke action depends on leverage to overcome the drag that is part of this largely underwater stroke. Leverage positively affects all aspects of breaststroke including the kick, arm stroke, recovery and breathing. Using the two balance points of the hips and the head, with the strong core in the middle, the swimmer can shift his or her balance, angling the body downward and upward in an alternating motion to achieve forward motion while minimizing drag. Use the following drills to improve your leverage in breaststroke.

## **68.** EXAGGERATED BREASTSTROKE

### The purpose of this drill

- Feeling the high point
- Feeling the low point
- Feeling the transitions

### How to do this drill

Step 1: In the water, begin in the breaststroke glide position. Sweep your hands out, then quickly in and back toward your chest as you draw your legs up and out in preparation to kick. Breathe and accelerate into your recovery. Kick. When your face begins to submerge, dive down deep into the water, exaggerating your downward balance point. Glide.

Step 2: Just before the momentum of your glide slows, begin your next arm stroke. From your deep position, your arm stroke must produce an exaggerated amount of lift to shift to the upward balance point. Sweep out quickly, then in and back even more quickly in order to get yourself up into breathing position.

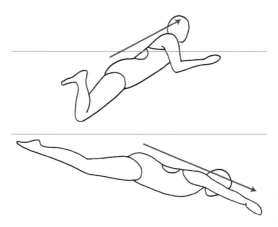

Step 3: Breathe within the recovery then kick with force. Feel your balance shift forward. Dive down and continue swimming breaststroke, exaggerating the balance points of the stroke.

*Figure 68: To feel leverage, exaggerate the high and low balance points of the stroke*

## Drill feedback chart

| PROBLEM | MODIFICATION |
| --- | --- |
| I float up when I am gliding. | You must produce more forward momentum to stay down. It should come from kicking with force. |
| From the exaggerated depth, I can't produce enough lift to breathe. | Keep trying. Feel the shift of your body balance upward and use it with your insweep to achieve more lift. |
| I am not maintaining a neutral chin position with the exaggerated breaststroke. | Use your body to shift your balance, not your head. |

# **69.** TEETER-TOTTER

## The purpose of this drill

- Avoiding swimming flat
- Feeling the shift of balance
- Establishing stroke rhythm

## How to do this drill

Step 1: Swim breaststroke focusing on the rhythm of the stroke. As you go through the arm stroke breathing, kick and glide motions of the stroke, feel your body shift between the upward and downward balance points. Notice how the rhythm of the breaststroke is defined by the highs and lows of the stroke.

Step 2: Swim breaststroke at a relaxed pace. Feel the rhythm of the stroke match the slow pace as your body leans towards the lower balance point, and then shifts to the upward balance point alternately, like the motion of a teeter-totter.

Step 3: Swim breaststroke at sprint speed. Feel the rhythm of the stroke speed up as your body leans towards the downward balance point, and then shifts to the upward balance point alternately like a teeter-totter.

Step 4: And like a teeter-totter that balances on a stable place in the middle, your hips remain stable as your extremities move up and down. Feel your chest and head shift from high to low. Feel your legs shift from low to high, in opposition to your chest and head. It is only when the teeter-totter balances flat that the rhythm

*Figure 69: Your hips remain stable as your extremities move up and down*

stops. Continue swimming breaststroke, avoiding swimming flat, and using your balance points to create rhythm for your stroke.

## Drill feedback chart

| PROBLEM | MODIFICATION |
| --- | --- |
| I feel flat when I glide. | Press your chest down as you hit the streamline position to achieve the downward balance point. |
| I lose my rhythm after a few strokes. | Use the glide phase to reset your rhythm with each stroke. |
| I still move forward when I swim flat. | Just think how much more distance per stroke you would get if you made use of the leverage from your core. |

# 70. BREASTROKE WAVE

## The purpose of this drill

- Utilizing the shift of balance
- Creating a forward wave
- Maintaining stable hips

## How to do this drill

Step 1: Swim breaststroke, shifting your balance to achieve the upward and downward balance points alternately through every stroke. Feel the rhythmic up and down movement of your stroke. Feel yourself stroke up and kick down.

Step 2: As you produce rhythm for your stroke by hitting the upward and downward balance points alternately, notice that you also achieve the other functions of the stroke simultaneously. As you perform the arm stroke and hit the upward balance point, you also inhale at the high point of the stroke. As you perform the kick at hit the downward balance point, you also position yourself for a productive glide.

Step 3: Try it again. Stroke up to breathe. Kick down to glide. Maintain your rhythm as you shift from up to down and down to up. Feel the forward wave you have created as you move through each stroke. Continue swimming breaststroke. Maintain your rhythm. Maintain your forward wave.

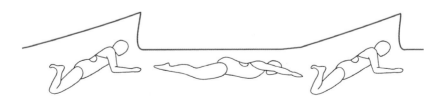

*Figure 70: Create a forward wave with your breaststroke*

## Drill feedback chart

| PROBLEM | MODIFICATION |
|---|---|
| I don't feel a forward wave, I feel an up and down wave. | The purpose of each movement up, and each movement down, is to help you move forward. Try to lean forward as you move up and down. |
| I get the feeling of stroking up to breathe, but not kicking down to glide. | Just before the power phase, drop your chest so your kick sends you forward and downward at the same time. |
| The rhythm I have is not even. | Good observation. Your time at the upward balance point should be shorter than at the downward balance point. This is the rhythm that should repeat every stroke. |

## 71. RIDE THE GLIDE

### The purpose of this drill

- Maximizing the glide
- Using momentum
- Understanding the benefit of the glide

### How to do this drill

Step 1: Push of the wall preparing to swim breaststroke. Stroke up to breathe, then kick, but do not glide. Instead, go immediately into the next stroke. Continue swimming breaststroke without a glide phase across the pool. Notice that you have to do a lot of strokes.

Step 2: Let's compare how many strokes it takes to cross the pool with and without a glide. Again, swim breaststroke across the pool with no glide following the kick. Count each stroke. Now swim breaststroke across the pool with a glide following the kick. Count your strokes. Notice that you do significantly more strokes without the glide, and it requires much more effort.

Step 3: Now compare how long it takes. Using a clock, time yourself swimming across the pool doing breaststroke with no glide. Time yourself again swimming across the pool with a glide. Notice that the time is the same or faster with a glide.

*Figure 71: Maximize your momentum in the glide*

Step 4: Continue swimming breaststroke, including the glide. Use the glide to cross the pool with less effort and more speed. Maximize your momentum with each stroke.

## Drill feedback chart

| PROBLEM | MODIFICATION |
|---|---|
| How long should I glide? | You should glide as long as it is productive. This means that you should start your next stroke before your glide momentum slows. If you wait until after you slow down, you will have lost the benefit of your glide, and will have to restart your forward motion with each stroke, which is a lot of extra effort. |
| My time is the same with and without the glide. | But you use less effort with the glide. So, work on improving your stroke with the glide, then re-compare. |
| I do the same number of strokes with and without the glide. | If you are not benefiting from the glide, check your kick productivity. Are you creating good forward motion with your kick? This is the main power in the breaststroke, and what propels you into your glide. |

## COORDINATION DRILLS

Even if every part of breaststroke is technically excellent, if they do not work together the breaststroke will not work well. Due to the many points of potential drag in the stroke and the overlapping sequence of the individual actions of the stroke, breaststroke must be well-coordinated, or the stroke will fight itself. Use the following drills to improve your coordination in breaststroke.

## **72.** 3-PHASE BREASTSTROKE

### The purpose of this drill

- Identifying the parts of breaststroke
- Sequencing breaststroke correctly
- Feeling the correct timing

### How to do this drill

Step 1: Swim breaststroke focusing on the parts of the stroke: arm stroke, breathing, kick and glide. Notice the sequence of these parts. Notice how they overlap. Notice which parts happen at the same time.

Step 2: Continue swimming breaststroke focusing on the arm stroke and breathing. Notice that they are so connected that they cannot be separated. Feel the unified movement of the arm stroke and breathing action. Consider the arm stroke and breathing as one part of the stroke.

Step 3: Continue swimming breaststroke focusing on the kick and the glide. Notice that they are separate actions. The glide follows the kick. Feel the cause and effect of the kick and the glide.

Step 4: Continue swimming breaststroke focusing on the three phases of the stroke in order as they happen: arm stroke

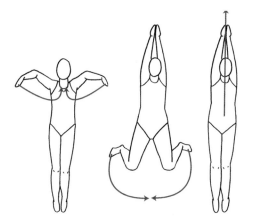

*Figure 72: Stick to the sequence of breaststroke: stroke and breathe, kick, and glide*

and breathing, kick, and glide. Maintain the sequence of the steps and you will maintain the correct timing of the stroke. Practice more.

## Drill feedback chart

| PROBLEM | MODIFICATION |
|---|---|
| What about the recovery, isn't that another step? | Good point. For the purposes of this drill, consider the recovery to be part of the arm stroke. In fact, the recovery is also connected to the breathing action, as the face returns to the water during the recovery. Think of the arm stroke, breathing and recovery as one step. |
| It seems that the kick begins before the breathing. | It is true that the heels begin to move into place for the power phase of the kick before the inhale, but the actual kick action, or power phase of the kick should happen after the breath. |
| I see the glide as an extension of the kick. | The glide certainly is propelled by the kick, but it is also affected by all the other parts of the stroke. If the other parts of the stroke, including the arm stroke and breathing, and the kick are not completed before the glide, the glide suffers from drag. For this reason, the glide should be considered a separate part. |

# 73. ARMS THEN LEGS

## The purpose of this drill

- Simplifying breaststroke
- Maintaining correct sequence
- Feeling productive breaststroke

## How to do this drill

Step 1. Swim breaststroke. Begin by sweeping out wider that the shoulders with the arms, then in and back towards your chest. Feel the balance of your body change as you do the insweep. Feel your face rise as you produce lift with the insweep. Inhale when your body achieves the upward balance point and draw your heels up and out and flex your feet. As your arms go through the recovery, let your face return to the water and move into the power phase of the kick as your balance shifts again. Achieve streamline with your arms then your legs and glide.

*Figure 73: To achieve the best glide, simplify the breaststroke to: arms then legs*

Step 2. Continue swimming breaststroke focusing on simplifying the many steps of the stroke. Perform the arm stroke and breathing, set the feet to kick, recover, kick then glide.

Step 3. Continue swimming breaststroke. Freeze at the point when your arms reach the extended position at the end of the recovery. Notice that at this point, your legs are beginning the power phase of the kick.

Step 4: Simplify the steps of breaststroke even more: arms then legs to achieve the best glide. Practice this simplified sequence of breaststroke for several laps.

## Drill feedback chart

| PROBLEM | MODIFICATION |
|---|---|
| My recovery is still in progress at the beginning of my kick power phase. | Try to accelerate the recovery more so it is finished by the time you start the power phase of your kick. This is important so that the movement of your recovering arms forward, and the movement of your kick back do not fight each other and produce drag. |
| My legs are not in position for the power phase until well after I have finished breathing. | Start drawing them back sooner so there is no downtime between the am stroke and the kick. Your legs should be in position, with your feet flexed as you inhale. |
| My arms start the next stroke before my kick is finished. | This leaves no window for the glide. Let your arms stop when they are extended. Then when your legs finish the kick, glide. The glide is the phase where you benefit from the effort your arms and legs have done in the previous stroke. Let the glide work for you. |

## 74. COUNTING BREASTSTROKE

### The purpose of this drill

- Getting back to streamline quickly
- Setting up to glide
- Maintaining good timing

### How to do this drill

Step 1: Swim breaststroke while you count the rhythm of your stroke. Use a eight-beat count for the entire stroke sequence, the first four beats counting the arm stroke and breathing, and the kick, and the second four beats counting the glide.

Step 2: Start by counting the arm stroke and breathing. Count "one" as you sweep your hands out. Count "two" as you sweep your hands in, inhale and raise your feet to kick. Count "three, four" as you recover, let your face submerge, and kick with force back and around. And as you glide, count "five, six, seven eight."

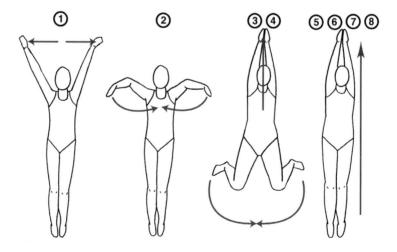

*Figure 74: Count the rhythm of breaststroke*

Step 3: Begin again. "One": sweep out. "Two": sweep in, inhale, and prepare to kick. "Three, four": recover, return your face to the water, and kick with force. "Five, six, seven, eight": Gli-i-i-i-i-i-i-i-ide. Practice several times. Spend as much time in the glide position as you spend to accomplish all the other steps in the stroke combined.

## Drill feedback chart

| PROBLEM | MODIFICATION |
| --- | --- |
| I can't get everything to happen at "Two". | You must be in the short float position and at the upward balance point at the same time. This way, your hands are close to your chest, your feet are close to your buttocks, and your face is out of the water simultaneously. |
| My kick lasts longer than one beat. | Kick back with more force both to produce good forward motion with your kick and to stay on time with your count. |
| My glide momentum ends before four beats. | Make sure you are producing a powerful kick. Also make sure that when you are gliding, you are leaning towards the downward balance point. |

# 75. BREASTSTROKE SILHOUETTE

## The purpose of this drill

- Being aware of your shape in the water
- Knowing the space you occupy
- Eliminating drag

## How to do this drill

Step 1: Swim breaststroke. Imagine you are watching yourself swim from above. Focus on your silhouette in the water in the glide position. Notice that it is long and narrow, and shaped to move through the water well. Now, focus on your silhouette in the water as you leave the glide position. Notice that you are shaped like a "Y"— not a position you want to stay in long if you are to maintain forward motion. Now focus on your shape as your hands finish the insweep. Notice that this is your shortest and widest position—the position to move through fastest in order to avoid drag. Finally, focus on your silhouette during the power phase of the kick. Notice that although your kick is wide, it is travelling fast, and your arms that make your leading edge are narrow.

Step 2: Swim breaststroke. Imagine you are watching yourself swim from the side. Focus on your silhouette in the water in the glide position. Notice that it is long and narrow, and shaped to move through the water well in a position aimed slightly downward. Now, focus on your silhouette in the water as you leave the glide position. Notice that although you are still long and narrow, your balance has shifted to an upward

*Figure 75: Keep your silhouette in mind and move through the drag points quickly to get back to your long, narrow floating position quickly*

floating position—not a position you want to stay in long if you are to maintain forward motion. Now focus on your shape as your hands finish the insweep. Notice that this is your shortest and most upward floating position—the position to move through fastest in order to avoid drag. Finally, focus on your silhouette during the power phase of the kick. Notice that your are again longer and shifting to float in the advantageous downward position.

Step 3: Keeping in mind your silhouette from above, and from the side, swim breast-stroke moving through the points of drag quickly and using your long, narrow downward floating position to your advantage.

## Drill feedback chart

| PROBLEM | MODIFICATION |
| --- | --- |
| From the top view I see that my elbows could cause a lot of drag at the insweep. | Remember that there has to be a good reason to leave the streamline position. In this case, if your elbows are high and wide because they are assisting in the lift of your upper body, than it is okay for them to be wide for a moment. If, though they are wide at the end of the insweep when there is no reason for them to be, fold them in to eliminate drag. |
| From the side, I see that the inhale position is when I take up the most room in the water. | Good observation. Once again, this is a necessary position, but one that you want to achieve quickly, and leave quickly to avoid as much drag as possible. |
| Gliding downward seems to take up more space in the water than gliding flat. | This is true, however there is more overall gain by gliding in this position than there is by gliding flat. |

# DRILLS FOR BUTTERFLY

## BODY POSITION DRILLS

Like breaststroke, butterfly body position depends on a shifting balance along the long axis of the body. And similar to breaststroke, the hips are at the center of this shift. But unlike breaststroke, the body position for butterfly must accommodate an over the water recovery and an arm stroke than extends to the hips, making body balance and counter balance a priority issue in this stroke. Use the following drills to improve your body position in butterfly.

# 76. ACTIVE FLOATING

## The purpose of this drill

- Learning to float actively
- Feeling core stability
- Learning to shift floating positions

## How to do this drill

Step 1: Take a big breath and float face down with your arms at your sides. Notice that your legs and hips begin to sink a bit, leaving your body floating uphill. This is an inactive floating position, and it not a position you want to stay in very long in butterfly.

Step 2: To change this floating position, actively lean forward until your feel that you are balancing on your chest. Your hips and legs should feel weightless and rise as a result. Maintain this position using core stability. This is the basic floating position for butterfly.

Step 3: Try it again. Float face down with your arms at your sides. Look at the bottom of the pool. Actively press down with your chest and lift your ribs slightly to shift your body position forward.

Step 4: Continue practicing. Alternately achieve the active floating position, then release it and allowing your body to

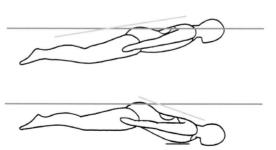

*Figure 76: Achieve the basic floating position for butterfly by actively leaning forward and balancing on your chest*

return to your inactive floating position. Spend more time in the active floating position.

## Drill feedback chart

| PROBLEM | MODIFICATION |
| --- | --- |
| When I press my chest down, my legs sink. | Isolate the movement of your upper body. Lean forward, rather than folding in the middle. |
| So, by pressing my upper body down in the water, my lower body floats higher. | Yes. By shifting your weight forward, the heaviest parts of your body—the hips and legs—act as if they are weightless. |
| Even when I press my chest down, my legs still sink. | Make sure you are looking at the bottom of the pool, and not forward. If your head is not in the right position, it can create imbalance in your stroke. |

## 77. HANG FROM YOUR HIPS

### The purpose of this drill

- Maintaining a high hip position
- Feeling the hips as the center of the stroke
- Establishing stability from the hips

### How to do this drill

Step 1: Take a big breath and float face down with your arms at your sides. Achieve the active floating position by leaning forward and balancing on your chest. Feel your hips and legs rise.

Step 2: Now, actively lean forward even more, until you are slightly bent forward at the hips and your chest and head are even lower in the water. Feel your hips and legs remain at the surface of the water. It should feel as though you are hanging from your hips. Maintain this position using core stability.

Step 3: Relax your pike and return to the original active floating position. Maintain core stability as you are coming out of the pike position. Continue practicing active floatation, hanging from your hips the whole time. First, actively lean forward and let your hips and legs be weightless. Then shift into the pike position with your legs and hips remaining at the water's surface. Alternate floating positions several times.

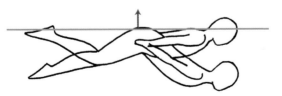

*Figure 77: Actively hang from your hips*

## Drill feedback chart

| PROBLEM | MODIFICATION |
| --- | --- |
| When I pike, my legs sink. | Imagine that your hips are weightless. As you lean forward with your upper body, let your legs be weightless too. |
| If I understand, it is only my upper body that moves when I change float positions. | Yes. The hips and legs should remain high in both floating positions. |
| When I change out of the pike position, my back hurts. | Make sure you are not lifting your head first, creating an arch in your back. Lift your head and upper body as a unit. |

# **78.** SHORT AND LONG BALANCE

## The purpose of this drill

- Feeling butterfly balance
- Feeling how float length changes balance
- Shifting floating balance

## How to do this drill

Step 1: Take a big breath and float face down in the water with your arms at your sides. Achieve a natural floating position by allowing your legs to sink slightly. This is the short float position.

Step 2: Again, take a big breath and float face down in the water, this time with your arms extended in front of you. Achieve the active floating position by leaning forward and balancing on your chest. With your arms extended, you will have to press your chest down more to shift your balance forward. Feel your hips and legs rise.

Step 3: As you lower your chest in the water, let your extended arms remain on the surface of the water, aiming forward, not down. Hang from your hips. This is your long float balance.

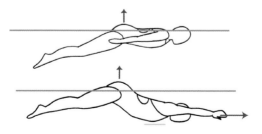

Step 4: Continue practicing both your long float and your short float.

*Figure 78: The short float aims up hill, the long float aims down hill*

## Drill feedback chart

| PROBLEM | MODIFICATION |
| --- | --- |
| I am not aimed down in my short float position. | No, in fact your body should be aimed slightly up hill. |
| I am aimed down in the long float position. | Your body should be aimed down—hips to shoulders, but your arms should be aimed forward at the surface of the water, and your legs should also be at the surface. |
| In both positions the hips are the highest point, correct? | Yes, the hips should remain in a stable, high position the whole time. |

## KICK DRILLS

The dolphin, used in the butterfly is more than a kicking action. It is a full body action that starts at the head and flows down through the legs. We see and feel the dolphin most in the legs, because it is moving at the greatest speed and with the greatest force by the time it gets down to the legs. But without initiating this action high in the body, the dolphin is much less powerful. So, when doing drills for dolphin, don't limit your focus to only the legs. Use the following drills to improve your dolphin technique in butterfly.

## 79. HEAD TO TOE DOLPHIN

### The purpose of this drill

- Feeling full body dolphin
- Initiating dolphin high in the body
- Flowing dolphin through the body

### How to do this drill

Step 1: Take a big breath and float face down in the water with your arms at your sides. Look at the bottom of the pool. Achieve the active floating position by leaning forward and balancing on your chest.

Step 2: From your active floating position, begin the dolphin by lowering your forehead, then your chin, then your chest, then flip that movement through your hips to your thighs, your knees and finally to your feet. Try it again with more speed. Create a whip like motion that starts with your head and moves with increasing speed and force through the length of your body and ends with a snap of your feet.

Step 3: Practice more. Notice that by the time you have transferred the dolphin action down to your hips, your upper body begins to rise, as the power continues to move down your legs to your feet.

*Figure 79: Initiate the dolphin high in the body and flip it down to your feet*

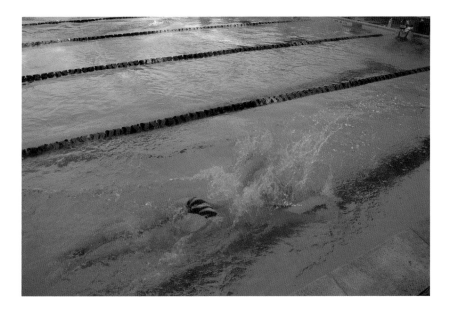

## Drill feedback chart

| PROBLEM | MODIFICATION |
| --- | --- |
| I cannot feel the dolphin flowing all the way down to my feet. | Practice more. Start slowly so you can get the sequence of movements, then gradually increase your speed, so that each of the individual movements will become joined together into one powerful motion by the time it gets down to your feet. |
| Do I lower my chest farther down than it already is in the active floating position? | Yes, momentarily, while the action flows through your chest. |
| I just keep going deeper with every kick. | When your dolphin flows past your hips, allow you head and chest to rise back to their starting position. This will keep you from descending deeper with each kick. |

## 80. NO BONES

### The purpose of this drill

- Achieving a fluid dolphin motion
- Feeling the wave of the dolphin
- Transferring power through your body

### How to do this drill

Step 1: Take a big breath and float face down in the water with your arms at your sides. Look at the bottom of the pool. Lean forward and balance on your chest. Begin the dolphin action by lowering your forehead, then your chin, then your chest, then send that movement through your hips to your thighs, your knees and finally to your feet.

Step 2: Try it again joining each movement together into a single fluid action. Forehead, chin, chest, hips, thighs, knees and feet. Feel the dolphin flow through your body as if you had no bones. Try it again with more speed, connecting each motion into a whip-like movement that gains speed and power from start to finish.

Step 3: Keep practicing. Create a wave that starts with your head and moves with increasing speed and force down your body and ends with a powerful snap of your feet. It should be fluid, with no major angles where you are joints are bending. Feel as if you have no bones as you send a fluid wave of power towards your feet.

Step 4: With each head-to-toe dolphin that you

*Figure 80: Create a fluid wave of dolphin as if you have no bones*

do fluidly, as if you had no bones, sending a wave of power to your feet, there should be forward motion produced. Each snap of your feet should propel you forward in the water. Feel the movement your dolphin produces.

## Drill feedback chart

| PROBLEM | MODIFICATION |
|---|---|
| When I get going fast, I can't tell where the beginning or the end of each dolphin is. | It sounds like you have succeeded in creating a wave-like action. To insure your wave produces forward motion, actively initiated each dolphin high in the body. |
| I feel boneless through most of the action, but I do get an angle at my knee. | If you bend your knee too much, the power of your dolphin will get stuck there. Try to flow the dolphin through your knee. |
| My dolphin stalls at my hips. | As the dolphin reaches your hips, allow them to rise and then snap them down quickly to flow the dolphin action to your lower extremities. |

# 81. HIGH / LOW

## The purpose of this drill

- Avoiding back strain
- Holding on to the wave
- Maintaining sequence

## How to do this drill

Step 1: Take a big breath and float face down in the water with your arms at your sides. Look at the bottom of the pool. Lean forward and balance on your chest. Begin the dolphin action by lowering your forehead, followed by your chin, then your chest, then send that movement through your hips to your thighs, your knees and finally to your feet.

Step 2: The dolphin ends when your feet snap downward. By that time your head and chest have risen back to their starting position. The wave you create with your head to toe dolphin always has one high end and one low end. Try it again. Feel the high and the low of the dolphin.

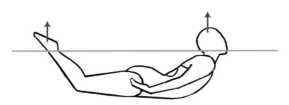

Figure 80a: Avoid back strain from moving your head and legs high at the same time

Figure 80b: The wave you create should have one high end and one low end, never two high ends

Step 3: To avoid back strain, never allow both ends of the dolphin to be up at the same time. When your head is down, your feet are up. When your head is up your feet are down. The motion should be stabilized by

233

your core and hips. Practice more achieving the high and low balance with each dolphin.

## Drill feedback chart

| PROBLEM | MODIFICATION |
| --- | --- |
| So, there is no arching of the back in the dolphin. | Correct. Not only is this hard on the back, it also stops the flow of the dolphin. |
| My head is still down when my feet snap down. | To get the full power of the dolphin to flow down to your feet, your head should be up when your feet snap down. Also, in order to produce a continuous dolphin action, your head should be back in its starting position to begin the next dolphin. |
| My back still hurts. | Try to use your abdominal muscles to stabilize your back. If you still feel pain, skip this drill. |

## 82. DOLPHIN WITH FINS

### The purpose of this drill

- Feeling fishlike
- Achieving forward motion from dolphin
- Feeling fluid dolphin action

### How to do this drill

Step 1: Wearing long fins, take a big breath and float face down in the water with your arms at your sides. Look at the bottom of the pool. Begin performing dolphin by lowering your forehead, your chin, your chest, then flow that movement through your hips to your thighs, your knees and finally to your feet. Notice that you create a very fluid, but narrow wave. Notice that your feet don't break the surface of the water. Continue practicing dolphin with long fins for several laps.

Step 2: Now wear short fins, and float face down in the water with your arms at your sides. Looking at the bottom of the pool, perform the dolphin by lowering your forehead, then your chin and your chest, then flow that movement through your hips to your thighs, your knees and finally to your feet. Notice that you create a very fluid and narrow wave. Notice that your feet don't break the surface of the water. Continue practicing dolphin with short fins for several laps.

Step 3: Finally, wearing no fins, float face down in the water with your arms at your sides looking at the bottom of the pool. Initiate the dolphin by lowering your forehead,

*Figure 82: Wearing fins allows you to feel the possibilities of the dolphin action.*

then your chin and chest, then flip that movement through your hips to your thighs, your knees and finally to your feet. Create a very fluid and narrow wave. Keep your feet attached to the water. Continue practicing dolphin without fins for several laps.

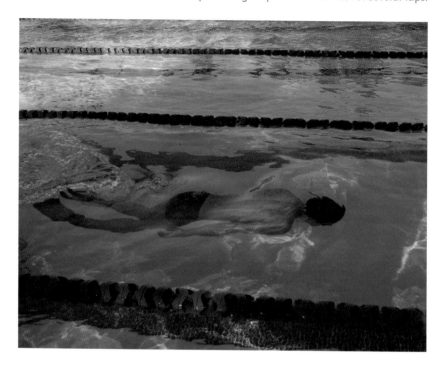

## Drill feedback chart

| PROBLEM | MODIFICATION |
|---|---|
| I can achieve a productive dolphin with fins. | Study it. What makes it productive? Duplicate the motion without fins. |
| My feet break the surface with fins. | This means you are bending your knees too much. |
| Long fins put a lot of stress on my back. | Try doing a narrower dolphin. Compact all of the power in your wave into a smaller vertical space. If it continues to hurt your back, skip this drill. |

## 83. SPIRALS

### The purpose of this drill

- Using core strength
- Controlling movement from the hips
- Maintaining fluid movement

### How to do this drill

Step 1: Float face down in the water with your arms at your sides looking at the bottom of the pool. Initiate the dolphin by lowering your forehead, then your chin and chest, then flip that movement through your hips to your thighs, your knees and finally to your feet. Create a very fluid wave. Repeat three times.

Step 2: After three productive dolphins on your front, roll to your right side and perform three more dolphins. Then, roll to your back and do three more dolphins. Then, roll to your back and do three more dolphins.

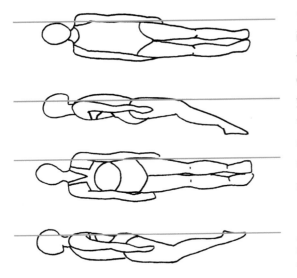

Step 3: Use your hips to initiate the roll. Maintain the same fluid wave, and continuous forward motion you achieve on your front when you are in the side or back floating positions. Continue doing dolphin spirals several times.

*Figure 83: Dolphin spirals help the swimmer feel core power and stability*

## Drill feedback chart

| PROBLEM | MODIFICATION |
| --- | --- |
| When do I breathe? | You can catch a breath when you roll to your back. |
| I go crooked. | This drill challenges you to initiate your roll from the hips, and to control your movements from your core. When you go crooked, it alerts you that something is not right. Make an immediate correction to your floating position, and keep going. |
| I go nowhere on my back. | It is the most difficult position, but by using the same sequence of movements, you can flow the power down to your feet. |

## ARM STROKE DRILLS

The powerful butterfly arm stroke is not as hard as it looks. It actually resembles freestyle in many ways, except that butterfly uses a simultaneous stroke, and therefore depends on long axis leverage, instead of the side-to-side roll of freestyle. The butterfly stroke gets its power from the center of the body, making the role of the hands simply to hold on to the water, rather than to lead the stroke. Use the following drills to improve your arm stroke technique in butterfly.

## **84.** PULL/PUSH BUTTERFLY

### The purpose of this drill

- Feeling the path of the arm stroke
- Transitioning from pull to push
- Accelerating through the arm stroke

### How to do this drill

Step 1: Stand in waist-deep water. Bend forward at the hips and extend your arms in front of you at about shoulder width apart. Submerge your face into the water and prepare to trace the path of the butterfly arm stroke.

Step 2: Pitch the palms of your hands slightly outward and sweep them to point just wider than your shoulders. Then, holding on to the same water in your hands, sweep your hands around and pull back towards your belly, and gather speed. Notice that your hands get closer together as move under your body. When your hands are at their closest point together, push back and out quickly from your hips to finish the arm stroke.

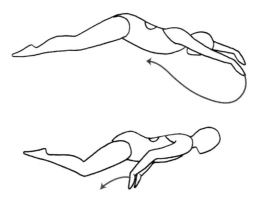

Step 3: Try it again. Set your arms in the water at about shoulder width and sweep your hands out and around, then pull under your body with increasing speed, keeping your elbows stable and high. When your hands are at their closest, push back and out quickly without losing momentum.

*Figure 84: When your hand reach their closest point together under your body push back and out quickl*

240

Step 4: Continue practicing the path of the butterfly arm stroke feeling the pull and the push of each stroke. Perform a pulling motion when your hands are in front of your shoulders. Perform a pushing action when your arms are behind your shoulders.

## Drill feedback chart

| PROBLEM | MODIFICATION |
|---|---|
| My hands don't get closer together under my body. | To achieve the strongest arm stroke, use a high, bent elbow position in the middle of the stroke, bringing your hands closer together. As your hands pass your belly they should be both closer together, and closer to your body. |
| Even though it changes in the middle, the pull is much longer than the push, correct? | Yes, the pull represents about two-thirds of the arm stroke, but the push is the fastest part. |
| I am losing momentum in the push. | This is an important point in the stroke to keep your speed up. Make sure that you are during the push phase you are pressing back and out, and not lifting the water up instead. |

## **85.** CATCH WIDE

### The purpose of this drill

- Finding the best catch position
- Feeling the water
- Setting the arms in the water

### How to do this drill

Step 1: Float face down in the water with your arms extended in front of you. Hook your feet over a lane line, or in the pool gutter. Prepare to practice the catch of the butterfly arm stroke.

Step 2: Achieve the active float position by lowering your chest in the water and maintain a high hip position. Although your body is aimed downward from the hips, keep your extended arms and hands at the surface of the water. Pitch your hands slightly palms-out and drive your chest down further resulting in your hands moving outward just outside your shoulders.

Step 3: From your wide set hand position at the surface of the water, press down on the water a few inches at the same time as you raise your chest slightly. This is the catch position for butterfly. Feel the water pressing against your hands. Feel how your wide hand position prepares you to gather the water and hold on to it throughout the arm stroke. Feel your body chest start to rise as you make your catch. Try it again several times.

*Figure 85: Drive your chest downward as you extend to a wide reach then feel your chest rise as you catch*

## Drill feedback chart

| PROBLEM | MODIFICATION |
| --- | --- |
| When I lower my chest, my hands also go down in the water. | Some swimmers are more flexible in the shoulders than others. The main thing is that your arms and hands should be as close to the surface as possible, and aiming forward, parallel to the surface, not down. |
| So, the butterfly catch is at the water's surface? | It is right under the surface of the water, as far as you can reach forward, and just outside your shoulders. |
| Why not just reach forward to catch? | With your arms extended, you are stronger from a slightly wider position. It is a major effort to vault your body through the water, you want to position yourself the best way possible to begin that effort. |

## 86. LEAN IN, LEAN OUT

### The purpose of this drill

- Feeling how body position affects the arm stroke
- Leaning in to the pull
- Leaning out of the push

### How to do this drill

Step 1: Swim butterfly. Extend your arms in front of you and press your chest down achieving an active floating position with stable, high hips. Do serveral dolphins in this position and make a wide catch with your hands near the surface of the water by pressing down on the water as your chest rises slightly. Sweep your hands back and around, pulling under your body as your chest rises. When your hands move close together under your belly feel your floating position change. Accelerate your arms into the push moving them quickly back and out from your hips as your chest rises to its highest point and your feet snap down.

Step 2: Try it again. Start by leaning into your stroke to catch and pull, then lean out of your stroke to push. Notice that your feet snap down at the conclusion of your full body dolphin as you lean into your stroke, helping you achieve depth with your chest. Notice that your feet snap down at the conclusion of your full body dolphin

as you lean out of your stroke, helping your chest achieve the highest point in the stroke.

Step 3: Again, lean forward to catch and pull, then lean out to push. Feel the

*Figure 86: Lean into your arm stroke to pull, lean out of your arm stroke to push*

dolphin flow through your body and snap through your feet as you lean into your stroke. Feel the dolphin flow through your body and snap through your feet as you lean out of your stroke.

Step 4: Continue swimming butterfly, leaning into and out of each stroke.

## Drill feedback chart

| PROBLEM | MODIFICATION |
|---|---|
| So, there are two dolphins for each stroke? | Yes. The first concludes at the feet as you are leaning into the stroke. The second concludes at your feet when you are leaning out of the stroke. |
| How does one dolphin move you up in the water, and one move you down in the water? | It is a matter of how your upper body is leaning. If it is leaning down, as when you catch and pull, then the dolphin assists you in that direction. If you are leaning up, as when you push to the back of the arm stroke, the dolphin assists you in that direction. |
| My hips sink when my chest is at the high point of the stroke. | Don't stay in the high chest position too long. Get your arms back to the front, and drop your chest. Keep your hips high throughout the stroke. |

## **87.** DEEP AND SHALLOW

### The purpose of this drill

- Feeling the deep and shallow points in the arm stroke
- Achieving a sweeping arm stroke
- Holding on to the water

### How to do this drill

Step 1: Swim six good butterfly strokes. Start with a few rhythmic dolphins then lean into your catch then pull around, back and inward under your body in a smooth, sweeping action. As you transition to the push, accelerate your arms as your body leans out of the stroke. Notice that your while you are leaning into your stroke and pulling, your arms travel deeper, and while you are leaning out of your stroke and pushing, your arms travel shallower.

Step 2: Rest, then swim six more good butterfly strokes. Lean in and pull deep, then lean out and push shallow. Notice that not only does your arm stroke follow a sweeping line from front to back, it also follows a sweeping line from deep to shallow.

Step 3: Continue practicing the sweeping arm stroke of butterfly, accelerating front to back and deep to shallow.

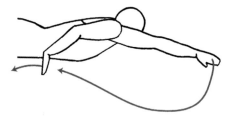

*Figure 87: Lean in and pull deep, then lean out and push shallow*

Drill feedback chart

| PROBLEM | MODIFICATION |
| --- | --- |
| To pull deep, should my arms remain straight? | No. The depth you achieve while you pull is not because your arms are straight, it is because your body is leaning into your stroke extending your reach. After you make your catch with your arms extended, almost immediately your arms begin to bend, and your forearms sweep down and inward while your elbows remain still and high. |
| To push shallow, my hands have to be very close to my body. | Yes. They are both close to your body, under your belly, and, close together. From there they push back and out from your hips. |
| It seems as well as deep to shallow, the arm stroke also goes from wide to narrow. | Good observation. It is like you are gathering the water inward and then vaulting over it. |

## 88. FINISH AND RELEASE

### The purpose of this drill

- Feeling the arm stroke's fast finish
- Feeling the direction of the push
- Learning to release the water

### How to do this drill

Step 1: Swim butterfly focusing on the transition from pull to push. Actively accelerate your motion towards the finish of each stroke. This is the fastest part of the arm stroke, and the part that produces the most lift. It is also the part that ends the arm stroke, signaling your hands to let go of the water. What is the best way to accomplish this?

Step 2: Try pushing the water back past your hips as in freestyle. Notice that your push produces a good surge forward for your body. Notice too that following the push, it is as if your arms get stuck at your sides underwater, leaving you unable to move into the next phase of the stroke.

Step 3: Try pushing the water back to your hips and then up to the surface of the water. Notice that your push back produces a good surge forward for your body. Notice too that the push upward, while accomplishing the task of getting your hands out of the water, is very difficult and slow because you are lifting water upward.

Step 4: Now try pushing the water back to your hips and then pressing your hands out away

*Figure 88: Finish each stroke by pressing back to your hips then out from your sides to release the water*

your sides. Notice that your push back produces a good surge forward for your body. Notice too that pressing out from your sides continues your surge forward while bringing your hands smoothly to the surface to easily release the water. Continue swimming butterfly, finishing each stroke by pushing back to your hips then out from your sides to release the water.

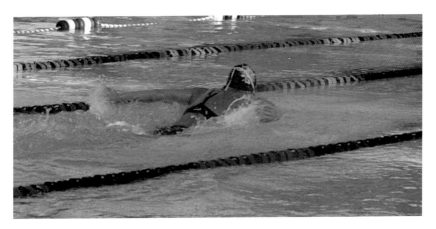

## Drill feedback chart

| PROBLEM | MODIFICATION |
| --- | --- |
| Doesn't finishing the stroke out from the sides make a shorter stroke? | It is not quite as long along the body, but the distance you push out is the same distance you would push back, and it not only produces the same forward motion, it allows you to release your hands from the water easily to move to the next stroke phase. |
| Why does pushing past your hips work in freestyle but not in butterfly? | Good question. Because of the rolling action in freestyle, the arm is able to finish the stroke while that side of the body is high in the water. In butterfly there is no such roll, so the finish must be handled differently. |
| Should I press out with the same speed as I press back? | Yes, it is a continuation of the fast finish. |

## RECOVERY DRILLS

Done well, the butterfly recovery is a dramatic sight that leaves no doubt that the swimmer knows what he or she is doing in the water. The characteristic double arm recovery of the butterfly is not only a way to get the arms back in position for another stroke, it can also add momentum, balance and alignment to the stroke. Use the following drills to improve your recovery technique in butterfly.

## **89.** ONE ARCH

### The purpose of this drill

- Feeling a unified recovery
- Using core strength
- Building momentum

### How to do this drill

Step 1: Stand in front of a full-length mirror. Bend forward at the hips. Extend your arms in front of you towards the mirror. Perform the butterfly arm stroke as if you were in the water. Catch wide and sweep your hands around and back and pull under your body, then push back and outward quickly to finish.

Step 2: Notice that at the very end of your arm stroke, when your hands push out to the widest point as if releasing the water, that a perfect arch forms from your left hand, up your left arm, through your chest and shoulders, down your right arm to your right hand. Move your arms forward into the recovery. Feel the power of your recovery arch.

Step 3: Try it in the water. Push off the wall with your arms extended and do several quick dolphins then lean into your wide catch and sweep the water around and back then pull under your body. Lean up and transition to the push back and out from your hips, then release the water to recover. Feel the strong arch form from hand to hand through your shoulders and chest.

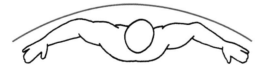

*Figure 89: Feel the power of your recovery arch connecting your arms in their path forward*

Step 4: Notice that as you are recovering, your arms feel connected throughout the movement. Notice that your powerful core is leading your arms. Feel the power from the middle of your recovery arch. Feel the momentum building as your arms travel back to the front. Practice for several laps.

## Drill feedback chart

| PROBLEM | MODIFICATION |
|---|---|
| My elbows drag through the water during my recovery. | As you are finishing the push outward, your hands are positioned in a pinkie up position. They should remain in that position as your hands leave the water and throughout the recovery. If your hands are in the pinkie up position, your elbows will not drag through the water. |
| I don't feel core leading my arms. | Try shrugging your shoulders up just a bit and then rolling them forward to lead your arms. Try this in the mirror first, then in the water. |
| My arms don't feel connected in the recovery. | Make sure you are not using your hands to initiate the recovery. Use the larger, stronger muscles at the top of your arms and shoulders to power this action. |

# **90.** HANDS FOLLOW

## The purpose of this drill

- Learning to lead from the core
- Relaxing your hands
- Feeling your hands follow

## How to do this drill

Step 1: Stand in waist deep water and bend forward at the hips until your face is submerged. Extend your arms in front of you. Trace the path of the butterfly arm stroke in the water. Catch, pull, and push the water back and out from your sides. Feel your hands emerge from the water.

Step 2: Looking at yourself in this position from above, you would see that your hands exit the water behind your shoulders, and your fingers would be pointing back towards your feet. Your hands should stay behind your shoulders through most of the recovery. Try the arm stroke and recovery again. Catch, pull, push, release. Feel your hands leave the water. Feel your hands follow your shoulders into the recovery.

Step 3: It is only after your arms reach the widest point in the recovery that your hands move ahead of your shoulders in order to line up for the entry. Try it again. At the finish of the arm stroke, as your hands release and emerge from the water, feel them relax, and trail the recovery, letting the larger muscles towards the middle of your body do the work.

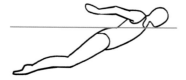

*Figure 90: The hands should follow the shoulders into the recovery*

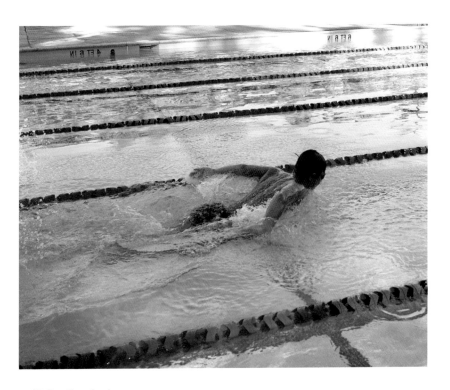

## Drill feedback chart

| PROBLEM | MODIFICATION |
| --- | --- |
| My hands don't follow, they lead. | Relax your hands from the wrist. Let them hang loosely while your shoulders and chest lead your arms through the recovery. |
| Should my elbows be bent during the recovery? | Some swimmers recover with straight arms, others recover with slightly raised elbows. In both cases, the hands should be the lowest part of the recovery. |
| So, my hands trail until my arms are at 90 degrees to my shoulders, then my hands lead, correct? | Yes. When your arms reach their widest point, at about 90 degrees to the body, then the hand reach for the front. |

## BREATHING DRILLS

The forward breathing style of butterfly can help or hinder the forward line of the stroke. Ideally, breathing should be done low to the water, and follow a parallel rise and fall to the arms. Good breathing in butterfly takes no independent action of the head because it happens when the upper body is at its highest point. It is only when breathing is timed incorrectly that it causes problems that can divert momentum away from the forward line, and interrupt the rhythm of the stroke that is extremely important to maintain. Use the following drills to improve your breathing technique in butterfly.

## 91. LOW PROFILE

### The purpose of this drill

- Maintaining the forward line of the stroke
- Inhaling with the face close to the water
- Keeping the rhythm of the stroke

### How to do this drill

Step 1: Swim butterfly. Feel the low and the high of each stroke. When your hands enter the water and catch wide, your head and chest are low in the water. When your arms are pushing fast and out from the hips, your head and chest are high in the water.

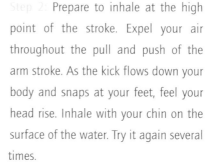

Step 2: Prepare to inhale at the high point of the stroke. Expel your air throughout the pull and push of the arm stroke. As the kick flows down your body and snaps at your feet, feel your head rise. Inhale with your chin on the surface of the water. Try it again several times.

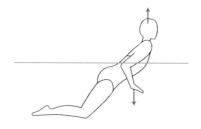

Figure 91b: Avoid trying to get high out of the water to breathe by pushing down on the water

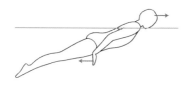

Figure 91a: Hold on to the forward line of your stroke by inhaling as the dolphin snaps down to your feet and your face rises

Step 3: Try to achieve the lowest profile breathing position possible. Avoid trying to get high out of the water to breathe by pressing down towards the bottom of the pool. You only need your mouth to clear the water. Hold on to your forward motion. Inhale with the downbeat of the kick as your hands push back and outward from your hips. Let the stroke's natural high point determine when you inhale. Practice more.

## Drill feedback chart

| PROBLEM | MODIFICATION |
| --- | --- |
| I am inhaling when my hands start the push. | Try to wait a little longer. Hold back on your inhale until your head is higher in the water, so you won't have to lift your chin and break the forward line of the stroke. |
| I am afraid if I don't lift myself higher to inhale, I will breathe water. | It is very important to use your stroke to move forward, rather than up. When you go up too much, you stop moving forward. Also, the more forward motion you create, the more the water will go by your mouth, not in it. |
| I feel a surge forward when I inhale. | Excellent! That means your timing is right. The inhale should occur simultaneously to the snap of the feet at the end of the dolphin, and the final push and fastest part of the arm stroke. These actions together produce the lift you need to breathe and the surge forward that you feel. |

# 92. TURTLE

## The purpose of this drill

- Lengthening the neck
- Maintaining the forward line of the stroke
- Inhaling low to the water

## How to do this drill

Step 1: Swim butterfly breathing each stroke. Inhale at the high point. Maintain your forward line in the water when your face rises by staying low in the water.

Step 2: To enhance your forward line while breathing, focus on your neck. When striving to inhale low in the water, it is common to raise the shoulders and let your neck and head retract between them. Instead, as your face emerges from the water, extend your neck forward like a turtle coming out of its shell. Try it several times.

Step 3: At the high point of the stroke, while you are breathing, keep your chin on the surface of the water. Let your neck be as long as possible, directing you forward while you inhale. Practice again. Observe the water you leave behind with each stroke from your low and longer breathing position.

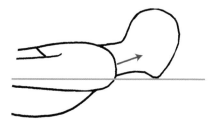

*Figure 92: As your face emerges from the water extend your neck foward*

**Drill feedback chart**

| PROBLEM | MODIFICATION |
|---|---|
| When I extend my neck my head tilts back. | It sounds like you are lifting your chin while you are elongating your neck. Isolate your neck muscles and try to keep your chin neutral. |
| When I extend my neck my face is even closer to the water. | Try extending the front of your neck rather than the back. |
| My shoulders are still tight and raised up. | Practice in the mirror keeping your shoulders low and relaxed at this point in the stroke. |

## 93. HEAD THEN HANDS

### The purpose of this drill

- Returning the head to the water early
- Maintaining the rhythm of the stroke
- Maintaining the forward line of the stroke

### How to do this drill

Step 1: Float face down in the water with your left arm extended in front of you and your right arm at your side. Swim butterfly with your extended arm only. Focus on achieving the high and the low point of the stroke. Focus on achieving a full body dolphin that flows down to your feet. Focus on maintaining high hips. Focus on the rhythm of the stroke.

Step 2: Now focus on your breathing. Inhale at the high point of the stroke, when your arms are pushing back to the finish. As your arms move forward into the recovery, let your face return to the water with them.

Step 3: Notice that while your face and your arms travel downward in unison, the path that your arms are traveling is much longer than that of the face. Continue swimming butterfly with one arm focusing on returning your face to the water with your recovering arms.

Step 4: While the face and the arms are moving back into the water at the same time, the relatively short path that the face travels back to the water, compared to the arms means that the face should enter the water an instant before the hands. Try it again, focusing on feeling your head enter the water and then your hands.

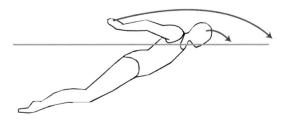

*Figure 93a: After inhaling, your face and recovering arms move back to the water together*

*Figure 93b: Because the path of your arms is longer, your face should enter the water before your arms*

Step 5: Now, swim butterfly with both arms. Focus on your face returning to the water after breathing at the same time that you are nearing the end of your recovery and your hands are preparing to enter the water. Feel that although both your face and your hands are moving together, because your face is closer to the water, it hits the water before your hands. Continue practicing, saying to yourself, "head, then hands."

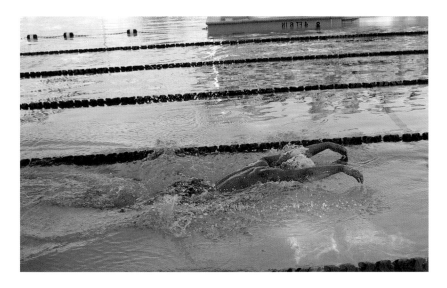

## Drill feedback chart

| PROBLEM | MODIFICATION |
|---|---|
| My head and hands hit the water at the same time. | Sometimes this results in your hands descending along with your head to a point that they are too deep to get a good catch. Keep working on getting your head down earlier. |
| My head is still up when my hands enter the water. | With this timing, you are canceling out your forward motion. In essence what is happening is your head is pulling you back while your arms are pulling you forward. It is important to get them moving forward together. |
| My head ends up at a lower position in the water than my hands. | That is fine. At entry, the hands should be stretched out on the surface of the water while the head is carried lower in the water by the descending chest. |

# **94.** BREATHING RHYTHMS

## The purpose of this drill

- Experiencing different breathing rhythms
- Maintaining stroke rhythm
- Holding the forward line of the stroke

## How to do this drill

Step 1: Swim butterfly without breathing. Perform as many good rhythmic strokes as you can. Focus on the forward line of your stroke. Without breathing, what happens at the high point of the stroke? The feet still snap down. The hand still move quickly back and out from the hips. But the face stays in the water. For some swimmers who produce good lift, it is actually an effort to keep their face down. They must lower their chin slightly and press their forehead into the water at the high point of the stroke to maintain stroke rhythm. For others, breathing is a taxing part of the stroke, and keeping their head down is welcome relief. However, breathing must be part of the butterfly if it is going to be sustainable for any distance.

Step 2: Swim butterfly breathing every third stroke. Two strokes without breathing, then one stroke breathing. This breathing rhythm may appeal to swimmers who find breathing to be an extra effort, but who recognize that they must breathe occasionally to fuel their stroke.

Step 3: Swim butterfly breathing every other stroke. One stroke without breathing, then the next stroke breathing. This breathing rhythm may appeal to swimmers who do not have strong feelings about breathing one way or another.

Step 4: Swim butterfly breathing every stroke. This breathing rhythm may appeal to swimmers who find breathing to be an integral part of the high point of the stroke.

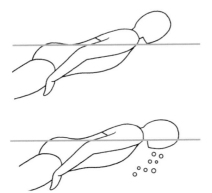

Step 5 Continue practicing different breathing rhythms for butterfly. Find the right one for you.

*Figure 94: Find the right breathing rhythm for you.*

## Drill feedback chart

| PROBLEM | MODIFICATION: |
|---|---|
| If you are not taking a breath at the high point of the stroke, what is the point of having a high point? | The wave motion of the butterfly affects more than breathing. It provides leverage at different points in the stroke, and it is part of the full body dolphin action. |
| So, on a non-breathing stroke, do you slow down your stroke at the finish and not snap your feet with as much force in order to make the high point lower? | No! Maintain your arm stroke speed and the powerful snap of your feet. The only thing that should change on a non-breathing stroke is that face stays in the water. |
| It is hard to keep the stroke rhythm when some strokes are breathing strokes and some aren't. | That is exactly the challenge. Keep practicing. If breathing is difficult to you, use a rhythm with a lot of breathing to get extra practice. If breathing is easy for you, use a rhythm that skips a number of breaths to get extra practice. Then, when you are comfortable with both, settle on a rhythm somewhere in the middle. |

## LEVERAGE DRILLS

Butterfly is all about leverage. Without it the stroke is very limited in terms of potential speed and power. Every aspect of the stroke depends on leverage to make it work, from the shifting body position, the dolphin action and the arm stroke to the breathing and coordination. With the hips as the center point of the stroke, leverage drives butterfly from the hips up, from the hips down, and through the length of the whole body. Use the following drills to improve your leverage in butterfly.

# 95. PIKE

## The purpose of this drill

- Feeling leverage high and low in the body
- Making use of leverage
- Using the hips as your fulcrum

## How to do this drill

Step 1: Swim several strokes of good rhythmic butterfly. Focus on hitting the high and the low of the stroke with your hips remaining high the whole time. Once you have established your stroke rhythm, freeze at the point when your arms are extended in front of you and your hands are making their catch to begin the next stroke. Notice that at this point in the stroke, both your chest and your feet are at their lowest point. It is almost as if you are hanging from your hips.

Step 2: Try it again. Swim several strokes, then when your arms stretched forward and catching the water for the next stroke, actively drop your chest down into the water, farther than it usually descends, and let the dolphin flow down to your feet and snap like the end of a whip. Notice that with your hips in theirs stable high position, and your chest dropped deeper than usual into the water, that your body is in a pike position, with your hips at the highest point, and your chest and feet both low. From this position, leverage works in two directions. First, your arm stroke is well set up to benefit from leverage from your core, and, at the same time that your dolphin will benefit from leverage as it flows from your hips to your feet.

*Figure 95: Your high hips make leverage possible both from the hips upward, and from the hips downward*

Step 3: Swim butterfly again. This time, rather than freezing as your hands catch the water, continue swimming. Focus on achieving a pike position in the water as your drop your chest and finish your dolphin with a snap. Then focus on the leverage that you produce by doing a bold pike both from the hips up, and, from the hips down as you continue through the stroke.

## Drill feedback chart

| PROBLEM | MODIFICATION |
| --- | --- |
| When I drop my chest farther than usual it breaks the rhythm of my stroke. | It changes your rhythm a bit, but it is worth it to gain more leverage for your stroke. |
| My feet have already kicked down when I am catching. | You get a better catch when the snap of the feet happens at he same time. Work hard to make this adjustment. |
| I don't feel the leverage work for my arm stroke. | Look for these point in your stroke: Right after you catch, your chest starts to rise as you arms start to pull helping you vault your body forward. And, as your arms pull under and closer to your body in the transition to push, your body shifts to a upward leaning position helping you move forward as your arms accelerate back and outward. These are two examples of leverage at work. |

# 96. THE MOTH

## The purpose of this drill

- Understanding the benefits of leverage
- Feeling the effects of leverage
- Maintaining rhythm and your forward line

## How to do this drill

Step 1: Instead of butterfly, swim the moth. The moth is butterfly with your hips as low as possible. Keep them low throughout the stroke. Attempt to perform all the actions of the stroke. Attempt to shift your body position. Attempt to do full body dolphin. Attempt to breathe. Notice that all of these actions are extremely difficult with low hips.

Step 2: Continue to swim the moth, focusing on the rhythm of your stroke. Notice that without the ability to easily shift your body position, you lose an important rhythmic element. Notice too that without the ability to flow your dolphin down to your feet, you cannot produce two evenly spaced kicks.

Step 3: Continue to swim the moth, focusing on the forward line of your stroke. Notice that with low hips, you must breathe up, rather than forward. Notice too that with low hips, your kick works to lift you up, not move your forward.

 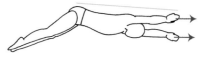

Figure 96a: The moth, or low-hip butterfly eliminates leverage opportunities and interrupts the rhythm and the forward line of the stroke

Figure 96b: Butterfly with a high-hip position makes leverage possible and maintains the rhythm and forward line of the stroke

Step 4: Now, swim butterfly with stable, high hips. Feel how the stroke actions are easier. Feel the rhythm of your stroke fall into place. Feel the forward line of your stroke return. Feel leverage in action.

## Drill feedback chart

| PROBLEM | MODIFICATION |
| --- | --- |
| I feel like I am going uphill the whole stroke. | Exactly. Butterfly is much harder without the leverage high hips make possible. |
| My feet come out of the water when I kick with low hips. | You have identified another problem. You have no choice but to over-bend at the knees when your hips are low. |
| My hands stall in front. | Yes, and when they stall you lose momentum and rhythm. |

## 97. KICK AND CATCH, KICK AND BREATHE

### The purpose of this drill

- Feeling leverage from the kick
- Maintaining stroke rhythm
- Keeping the forward line of the stroke

### How to do this drill

Step 1: Swim butterfly focusing on the rhythm of the kick, specifically when the feet snap down at the end of the dolphin. One happens at the beginning of the stroke, the other happens at the end. The kicks have a very predictable rhythmic because they are evenly spaced within the stroke.

Step 2: Continue swimming butterfly focusing on the catch of the stroke. This very important action initiates each stroke when the hands get a firm grip on the water. Notice that your feet snap down at the same time as you catch giving you a better handle on the water. Try it again. Feel the benefit of the kick as you catch.

Figure 97a: The downbeat of the first dolphin should happen as you catch

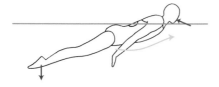

Figure 97b: The downbeat of the second dolphin should happen as you breathe

Step 3: Continue swimming butterfly focusing on the breathing action. At the natural high point of the stroke, the face rises for the inhale. Notice that your feet snap down at the same time as you inhale, giving you lift to clear your mouth from the water. Try it again. Feel the benefit of the kick as you breathe.

Step 4: Rest then swim butterfly again establishing a stroke rhythm by saying to yourself, "kick and catch, kick and breathe." Repeat several times.

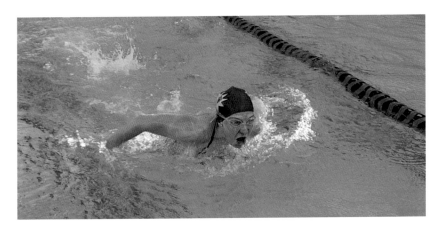

## Drill feedback chart

| PROBLEM | MODIFICATION |
|---|---|
| My kicks are not evenly spaced. | A common problem is to have two kicks when your hands are in the front of the stroke, and none in the back of the stroke. This happens when there is a stall at the front of the stroke, usually due to the arms entering too close to the centerline, so extra time must be spent getting the hands out to the catch position. By maintaining a wide entry, this stall can be eliminated. |
| If I understand correctly, one kick gives you lift and the other gives you depth. | More precisely, one kick moves you up and forward, the other one moves you down and forward. |
| This drill requires that I breathe every stroke. | You can also time the kick to the finish of the arm stroke if you prefer. "Kick and catch, kick and finish." |

## COORDINATION DRILLS

Contrary to popular belief, butterfly is more a matter of coordination than strength. While it is possible to simply power through the various actions of the stroke, it soon becomes very tiring. When these stroke actions work together butterfly is not only more graceful, it is more effective. By using the correct sequence and timing of stroke elements, butterfly becomes a sustainable stroke. Use the following drills to improve your coordination in butterfly.

## 98. GRAB AND GO!

### The purpose of this drill

- Avoiding a stall at the front of the stroke
- Maintaining stroke rhythm
- Making use of momentum

### How to do this drill

Step 1: Swim butterfly for several laps without stopping. Swim until your stroke feels tired. As you fatigue, notice how the quality of your stroke deteriorates. Notice exactly what happens. Your stroke rhythm suffers as your hands stall in the front of your stroke. When your hands stall you eventually end up doing two kicks at the front of the stroke. When you do two kicks at the front of the stroke you lose momentum to finish your stroke fast and to breathe.

Step 2: Swim butterfly again. Eliminate any stall at the front of your stroke that will cause your rhythm to suffer. As your hands enter the water wide and shallow, extend your arms and grab hold of the water, immediately sweeping into your pull. Grab and go!

Step 3: Now swim butterfly very fast for a short distance, increasing the tempo of your stroke as much as possible. Grab and go with every stroke. Notice that when your hands do not stall at the front of your stroke that your kicks are spaced evenly through the stroke. One kick in front, one kick in back. Notice that when your kick rhythm is even the finish of your stroke is much more effective, and your inhale is much less effort.

*Figure 98: Avoid stalling with your hands at the front of the stroke... grab the water and go*

Step 4: Continue practicing grab and go butterfly. Feel the momentum at the beginning of the stroke benefit the stroke actions that follow.

## Drill feedback chart

| PROBLEM | MODIFICATION |
| --- | --- |
| When my hands stop at the front of the stroke, I get rest! | Unfortunately, resting at the beginning of the stroke starts a downward spiral for the butterfly. After your rest, in effect you must restart your stroke because you have lost all of your momentum. This makes each stroke harder and harder, so you will need to rest longer and longer at the beginning of each stroke. Wait until you are finished swimming butterfly to rest. |
| It is hard to space out my kicks. | If your arms move quickly through the beginning of the stroke, there will only be time for one kick. By the time your feet are ready to kick down again, your arms will be near the finish of the stroke where the next kick is supposed to happen. |
| This quicker rhythm makes me tired sooner. | At first it will be more tiring because you aren't used to it. But with practice, you will get to the point where it actually feels easier than butterfly with a stall in the front. |

# 99. WEIGHTLESS FLY

## The purpose of this drill

- Feeling light in the water
- Feeling high in the water
- Maintaining stroke rhythm

## How to do this drill

Step 1: Swim butterfly across the pool. Imagine you are swimming in a pool that is only two feet deep. You must achieve the high and the low of the stroke within this space. You must perform the deep to shallow arm stroke within this space. You must achieve a full body dolphin that flows down to your feet within this space.

Step 2: You must accomplish all the actions of butterfly in very little depth. To achieve this you must stay near the surface of the water, as if you were weightless. Make each of your stroke actions count. Practice more concentrating the effect of each action into less space.

Step 3: Swim butterfly across the pool again. Be light. Be high in the water. Make every action quick and narrow. Make every action connect to the next. Make every action count.

*Figure 99: Accomplish all the actions of butterfly within very little depth*

## Drill feedback chart

| PROBLEM | MODIFICATION |
| --- | --- |
| How can I get the same effect in less space? | Use quick, precise and connected movements. Achieve all the actions of the stroke by utilizing leverage effectively throughout the stroke, and swimming high in the water as if you were weightless. |
| My body position shifts are very minor. | They can be minor in depth without being minor in effectiveness. Practice packing all of the leverage that happens as your body position shifts into a smaller space and time. |
| How do I know if I have succeeded? | You will have the feeling of weightlessness while moving forward. |

# 100. FULL BODY FLY

## The purpose of this drill

- Connecting stroke actions
- Feeling power from the core
- Utilizing momentum

## How to do this drill

Step 1: Swim butterfly across the pool. Achieve the high and the low of the stroke. Catch, pull and push. Recover in an arch over the water. Send your dolphin action from high in your body down to your feet. Catch and kick, breathe and kick.

Step 2: Notice what parts of the body you are using to move forward in the water. Your head leads the stroke, providing alignment and balance. Your neck extends during breathing to further the forward line of the stroke. Your shoulders create a bridge of strength between the arms that work as unified force. Your hands catch and hold on to the water through the sweeping pull and push of the stroke. Your chest rises and falls as one of your lever points. Your core sends power to all four limbs. Your hips stay high and act as the fulcrum of the stroke. Your legs receive the dolphin action started high in your body and flow it to your feet that carry all of the energy built in the body into a quick downward snap.

Step 3: Swim butterfly across the pool again feeling every part of your body contribute to the forward motion of the stroke. Feel the chain reaction of stroke actions as you swim. Feel all your power radiate from your core. Practice more.

*Figure 100: Feel every part of your body contribute to the forward motion of the stroke*

## Drill feedback chart

| PROBLEM | MODIFICATION |
|---------|--------------|
| How does your head provide alignment and balance? | By keeping your head in a neutral position, it does not interrupt the forward line of the stroke. By keeping your head low, it does not interfere with the high and low of the stroke. |
| How are your hips the fulcrum of the stroke? | They are at the center of the butterfly action. Leverage occurs from the hip upward, from the hips downward, and from head to toe, with the hips stable and high in the middle. |
| I feel a break in the chain reaction of stroke actions as my recovery begins. | Your core is the unifying factor. Use its power throughout the stroke. Analyze where you experience the break, then practice connecting that motion and the one before it to the core. |

# CONCLUSION

Now that you have made it to the end of this book, your mind is probably reeling from all the drills you have absorbed, and from the exciting possibilities of improving your swimming technique. Now it is time to get in the pool and put it to use.

Keep thinking about what you are doing. Focus on the point of each drill that you do. It is all about that mind/body connection.

Practice often and practice correctly. Repeat drills over several swim sessions until they feel natural and make sense.

Be patient and enjoy the process. Celebrate your results.

# CREDITS

**Illustrations** by Blythe Lucero
**Photos** by Kurt Krueger and Blythe Lucero
**Photos** by © Thinkstock/iStockphoto: p. 5, p. 14-15, p. 18-19, p. 26-27, p. 32-33
**Cover photo** by © Thinkstock/iStockphoto

**Swimmers pictured in photographs:** Meredith Anderson, Pam Bennett, Cornelia Bleul-Gohlke, Jonas Brodin, Katherine Cohen, Monique Commachio, Sara Ebadi, Annie Fujimoto, Liam Godfrey, Bill Grant, Katie Grue, Cory Haarke, Caroline Howard, Laura Howard, Ellen Johns, Eric Johnson, Monica Lam, Siobhan Langlois, Bonnie Lucero, Elise Lusk, Adrian Murillo, Alissa Perrucchi, Eric Rhodes, Meg Shean, Dove Shearer, Lisa Suden, Spencer Tuma, Josh Wang, Ian Umemoto

**Editing** by Sabine Carduck and Manuel Morschel
**Copy Editing** by Sebastian Meyer
**Cover & Book layout** by Claudia Lo Cicero

# FURTHER BOOKS
# BY BLYTHE LUCERO

Blythe Lucero

## 100 BEST SWIMMING DRILLS

Drill practice is a swimmer's primary tool in developing better stroke technique, allowing them to concentrate on a single aspect of a stroke at one time. By providing specific, repetitive practice and immediate feedback, drills teach a swimmer to maximize efficiency while minimizing effort.

3rd edition

280 p., in color,

133 photos, 131 illus.,

Paperback, 6 ½ x 9 ¼

ISBN: 9781841263373

$19.95 US/$32.95 AUS

£14.95 UK/€19.95

Blythe Lucero

## STRENGTH TRAINING FOR FASTER SWIMMING

In order to enhance your performance, swimming alone is not enough. An effective strength training is crucial if you want to improve your swimming times. This book shows you what types of strength training benefit swimming and how to develop a winning routine. It includes swim-specific strength training and lots of sample workouts.

168 p., in color,
115 photos, 48 illus.,
Paperback, 6 ½ x 9 ¼

ISBN: 9781841263397

$16.95 US/$29.95 AUS
£12.95 UK/€16.95

**MEYER & MEYER Verlag**
Von-Coels-Str. 390
52080 Aachen
Germany

Phone    +49 02 41 - 9 58 10 - 13
Fax       +49 02 41 - 9 58 10 - 10
E-Mail    vertrieb@m-m-sports.com
E-Books   www.m-m-sports.com

All books available as E-books.

MEYER
& MEYER
SPORT

# SWIMMING IN
# EVERY SITUATION

Ingrid Loos Miller

## FEARLESS SWIMMING
## FOR TRIATHLETES

IMPROVE YOUR OPEN WATER SKILLS

"Fearless Swimming for Triathletes" will help triathletes overcome the real and imagined threats of swimming in a chaotic, unfamiliar environment. This guide addresses a triathlete's concerns in a progression of skills to take the athlete confidently from pool to lake to river to sea.

2nd edition

168 p., in color,

29 photos, 15 illus., 14 charts

Paperback 6 ½" x 9 ¼"

ISBN: 9781841261201

$ 18.95 US/$ 32.95 AUS

£ 14.95 UK/€18.95

Dabrowska/Peszek

## LITTLE SWIMMER

For children, swimming is an opportunity to develop both physically and mentally. This book gives tips on how to prepare a child for a visit to the swimming pool and how to make every visit safe. A large part has been devoted to games in the water with children between 3 months up to 4 years of age.

c. 150 p., in color,
c. 300 illus. and photos,
Paperback, 6 1/2" x 9 1/4"

ISBN: 9781782550129

c. $16.95 US/$29.95 AUS
£12.95 UK/€16.95

**MEYER & MEYER Verlag**    Phone    +49 02 41 - 9 58 10 - 13
Von-Coels-Str. 390    Fax    +49 02 41 - 9 58 10 - 10
52080 Aachen    E-Mail    vertrieb@m-m-sports.com
Germany    E-Books    www.m-m-sports.com

All books available as E-books.

MEYER
& MEYER
SPORT